Get the Edge at Low-Limit Texas Hold'em

A Scoblete Get-the-Edge Guide

Get the Edge at Low-Limit Texas Hold'em

From the Kitchen to the Cardroom!

by Bill Burton

Foreword by Frank Scoblete

Chicago and Los Angeles

08 07 06 05 04   7 6 5 4 3

Library of Congress Control Number: 2002114959
ISBN: 1-56625-189-3

Bonus Books
875 N. Michigan Ave., Ste. 1416
Chicago, Illinois 60611

Printed in the United States of America

Dedicated To
My loving wife Sandy

In Memory Of
Bill "Pop" Ferguson
His love for cards was exceeded only by his love for his family.

Table of Contents

Foreword

by Frank Scoblete

Bill Burton is the "everyman" of low-limit Texas Hold'em; that is, if everyman is a disciplined, tenacious, and studious winner. If you're reading this book, it is possible that you are looking to engage in the casino poker wars for the very first time. Or, it is possible that you have been getting burned time and again on your trips to the cardrooms and you have decided that it is about time you learned what you were doing wrong. It is even possible that you are a veteran low-limit player looking to finally marry the theory and practice of Texas Hold'em to your own game or renew your vows to strong play.

Regardless of which category you fall into, *Get the Edge at Low-Limit Texas Hold'em* can help you. Not only is it a detailed, intelligently balanced course in how to play a winning game of Texas Hold'em, it is also a beautiful account of how an ordinary man, of extraordinary will power, became a successful low-limit player.

Bill Burton has been a friend of mine for years now but I knew him "when"—when he was just a regular casino player bucking the inevitable house edges at games where the casino will ultimately have the last financial say. His journey from average player to knowledgeable and respected expert has been dramatic and, in the scheme of things, like lightning. He is the casino guide for About.com, one of the most popular Web sites for information about anything and everything. His weekly casino gambling columns are informative and well-written. Bill is an excellent researcher and, when he sets his mind to learn something, he is dogged in his tenacity to master that something.

So it was with Texas Hold'em.

Bill was determined to become a winning casino gambler. He first tackled blackjack and card counting; but he felt that today's blackjack games were only marginally beatable by card counting (at best) and even those that could be beaten offered the expert player the dismal possibility of being "asked" to leave the casino by a pit boss or shift manager or the equally dismal possibility of having the casino boss flatter you with, "Sir, your blackjack play is too strong for us but you're welcome to play any game in our casino but blackjack." If you enjoy the casino culture such a prospect can sour the experience.

Bill then turned to video poker, a game he still plays and enjoys, but unlike most video poker players who will play any and almost all machines, Bill found the right machines and the right strategies to play those machines so that with proper play and some comps along the way, he had a positive expectation.

Still, video poker is not dynamic; you play by rote and win over the long haul by adhering to the underlying nature of the mathematics of that game. Play positive payback machines and, in the long run, you'll win whatever the percent of your edge is on the game and whatever the comps are that you have from the casino based on your total action. There's no room for inspiration or, frankly, thought, once you learn the proper play of the hands.

Not so with Texas Hold'em. This is a live game, against living opponents; a game of proper strategy, yes, but also a game in which you must out-think the other players. In fact, playing each and every hand the exact same way each and every time, as you do in video poker, is probably a mistake for, as Bill shows in this book, astute players can get a read on you and beat you because of that.

Texas Hold'em is a game of understanding positioning, understanding proper strategy for that positioning, understanding odds, understanding your opponents' psychology, and understanding yourself. It is dynamic, often dramatic.

And it is a game that, with proper condition and practice, can be a money winner for good players. That's right. If you follow Bill Burton's advice and his example, you can become a winning player. What's more, no casino boss will tap you on the shoulder and say "you're too good"; no one will "ask" you to leave the establishment; instead of being treated like the underbelly of humanity for your skill, as expert card counters are often treated, you will be a king or queen of the poker rooms.

Whether you play blackjack for $5 or $500; whether you play video poker for 25¢ or $25, your decisions will always be the same, if the game is the same. But in Texas Hold'em, playing for low stakes is often a radically different game than playing for high stakes. The reason for this is simple—the players you will often find at the low stakes games will make moves that a high-stakes player rarely makes. They stay in on more hands; there are more showdowns at the end of the game. It's tougher to bluff them. You have to have a certain mindset to play against them, a somewhat different mindset than you might need against high-stakes players.

But first things first. To be a successful Texas Hold'em player, you have to know what hands to play and when and how to play them. This book is not a one-read-and-you-too-can-be-an-expert kind of book. You might find that you'll want to read and reread many of the chapters. I recommend that you underline salient points; that you ponder the questions that this game poses. I also recommend that you follow Bill Burton's advice about how to learn. If you have never played Texas Hold'em in a casino before, then do exactly what Bill did—study, practice, and study some more—before you put your hard-earned money on the table. When you have played, then analyze your previous play and be, as Bill says, brutally honest with yourself. Learn your weaknesses and understand how to exploit your strengths. And never play just to be in the action—that way lies disaster.

One more thing to remember about casino players in general and, perhaps, low-limit poker players in particular—very few are really serious about their vocation and many don't bother to really learn the ins and outs of the games they play. In poker, that means the astute player will get an edge over the other players, an edge that means money in the bank. It takes work, of course, but very few things that are worthwhile are effortless. Make the effort here and you'll meet with success.

See you in the cardrooms!

Acknowledgments

My biggest concern in writing the acknowledgments for this book is possibly leaving out someone who I should mention. There were many people who helped me along the way while I was learning to play Texas Hold'em and while I was writing this book. I apologize if I have inadvertently left out anyone. All I can say is that you know who you are and I appreciate your help.

First and foremost I would like to acknowledge Scott Kurnit and Bill Day, founders of The Mining Company which would eventually become About.com. Years ago when the Internet was new they had the vision of starting a company utilizing live "guides" to help people find their way around the Internet. Not only did they create one of the today's most popular Internet Portals, but also they opened a new venue for many talented writers to showcase their work. When I signed on in 1998 there was little opportunity for a new gaming writer to break into the market. I thank them for giving me the opportunity to develop the Casino Gambling Site, and their continued support over the years.

When I decided to learn how to play casino poker for a series of articles I was writing, I turned to the Gamblers Book Shop in Las Vegas for help in researching the game. I met with Peter Ruchman and Howard Schwartz. Although they had never met me, they invited me to stop and discuss my project with them. They were most generous with their time and advice. I have met with them on numerous occasions since then and I am honored to consider them amongst my friends.

I would like to thank my friend and co-worker Jack Ambrosi for helping me understand the procedures and protocols of the poker room. Jack's advice took away any apprehensions I had about trying my hand at casino poker. Our discussions about Texas Hold'em has helped me improve my game.

Later in this book I discuss networking with other players. I would like to thank several members of my poker network, which consists of a group of players who participate in e-mail discussions about Texas Hold'em. John DeRose, Mike Bunkers and Ray Bilodeau helped with reading my original manuscript and offering advice and suggestions for improving it. Joining these three in our poker discussions are Andrew, Grant, Svetlanka, Capt. Jack and a few others who wish to remain anonymous. Together we have helped each other improve how we play the game. A special thanks goes to Bob Convertito for giving me a novice's critique of this manuscript.

I want to thank Bob Wilson for supplying me with the latest updates of his Turbo Texas Hold'em software. The program was a valuable tool in helping me learn to play the game correctly

Frank Scoblete is the top gaming writer in the country and it was an honor to be asked to write one of the books in his Get-the-Edge series of books. I want to thank Frank for his help with this project and his encouragement. More than that I wish to thank him for his friendship over the years and the good times we have had in the casinos.

Finally I would like to thank my loving wife, Sandy. Without her support and love, writing this book would never have been possible.

Part One

Introduction

Chapter 1

Is This Book for You?

Would you like to learn how to play winning low-limit Texas Hold'em? Have ever you thought about playing poker in the casino but were not sure if you could compete? If your answer to these two questions is "Yes," this book is for you.

I am not a professional poker player. I am the Casino Gambling Guide for About.com (*http://casinogambling.about.com*). I made my first trip to the casino over 20 years ago. Since that time I learned how to play every casino game except live casino poker. I have been writing a weekly column about the casinos and the games on the About.com casino gambling Web site since 1998.

I started receiving questions about casino poker from the readers of my column. I grew up playing kitchen-table poker and had some experience playing in the Friday night games with the guys in college but I had never ventured into the casino poker room. I felt it was time to learn how to play. I sought out the advice of Peter Ruchman and Howard Schwartz at The Gambler's Book Shop in Las Vegas. After discussing the games with them, I decided to learn how to play Texas Hold'em. I had never played this game and was looking forward to the challenge.

In January 2000, I started my project to learn how to play Texas Hold'em. I developed a training program for myself to follow. I took the time to study the game before I ever sat down at a table in the casino. From my very first game, I started winning playing $3/6 Hold'em. Of course I did not win every session, but at the end of the first year my logbook verified that I had a winning record. Shortly after I started playing, I noticed that there was a large number of low-limit players who either have no knowledge of the concepts for correctly playing the game or they just lack the discipline to apply them. I quickly learned to take advantage of this situation at the tables.

While I was learning the game, I started to participate in low-limit Hold'em tournaments as well. My goal was to make it to the final table by the end of the year. In May 2000, I accomplished that goal and set another one to win the tournament by year's end. The following month on June 19th, I captured first place in the weekly tournament at Foxwoods Casino in Connecticut, beating 78 other entrants. Two weeks after that I repeated the win, besting 74 players. I knew my method of learning was working and I was becoming a successful Texas Hold'em player.

Winning Is the First Step

The ultimate goal when playing poker is to maximize your profits. You can't do that until you first learn how to play winning poker. I honestly believe that a player with average intelligence and above average desire to succeed can learn to play winning poker. If you are a new player this book will give you the information needed to play winning Texas Hold'em in the casino. If you presently play, but have not been having the desired results, this book will take you back to the basics needed to play a solid game. But winning does not come without a price. You will have to make a serious effort if you hope to succeed.

In this book, I have documented the steps I have taken to learn how to play and win at Texas Hold'em. The information in this book will give you a strong foundation to build your winning game upon. It highlights key points that you will need to know if you are to succeed. I will also share some of the mistakes that I have made along the way so hopefully you can avoid them.

Will Reading This One Book Guarantee That You Will Be Successful?

Absolutely not! And I would not insult your intelligence by even suggesting that it would. No book can do that. It will take hard work and dedication on your part if you wish to succeed. There will also be additional reading that I recommend. If you were to attend college it would take more than reading one book to earn your degree. Winning players learn to assimilate information taken from many sources and adjust it to their own style of play. Consider this book your freshman primer to playing winning poker. It will be your road map on your journey to becoming a successful player. The information offered here will get you started playing winning low-limit poker. It will be up to you to take it to the next level.

There is one thing that you need to know before you even consider playing Texas Hold'em in the casino. You will need patience and discipline to be a winner. In low-limit games many players play "No Fold'em Hold'em." If you learn the proper starting hands and have the discipline to wait for them, you will be far ahead of the average player you will meet at the tables.

Are you the type that craves action and wants to jump in and mix it up with the other players believing that any two cards can win? If so, save your money. This book is not for you and you will need all your money at the tables.

I started my project in order to experience playing casino poker. My goal was to learn enough so I would be comfortable sitting at a table, and hopefully play well enough to be competitive. What I found was a game that would allow me to make money. The training methods I used were successful and I found that not only was I able to compete, but there were many bad players that I could exploit for my own financial gain.

I have heard many player's say "I'd rather be lucky than good." This is nonsense! I'd rather be knowledgeable than lucky. Lightning does occasionally strike, and so does the miracle flop that will turn garbage into gold but you can't depend entirely on luck if you want to win consistently. When I started writing my weekly gaming column for the About Casino Gambling Web site. I adopted a motto that appears at the end of all my articles:

Luck comes and goes . . . knowledge stays forever.

Are You Ready to Learn How to Play Winning Low-Limit Texas Hold'em?

You don't have to know a thing about Texas Hold'em but you should have a general knowledge of how poker is played. If you have ever played kitchen table poker you meet all the prerequisites. This book will help you make the transition from the kitchen to the cardroom.

Read on.

Chapter 2

Becoming an Educated Player

I grew up in a card playing family. I recall many Sunday afternoons when the adults would clear away the dinner dishes and break out the poker chips for an afternoon game. As a kid I was fascinated with the game and would pull up a chair to watch the action. As I got older, I would sit in on a hand when someone took a break. It was a rite of passage when I was finally allowed to pony up my 50¢ for chips and take a seat at the table. We played draw, stud and all the wild games such as baseball and deuces wild that you find in your typical kitchen-table games.

When I went away to college I could always find a game in the dorm. After college I would occasionally play in games on Friday or Saturday night with the guys. Unfortunately, as time went on, the poker games were becoming less frequent. After I learned to play casino games properly home poker games lost their glamour. They could not compete with the excitement of the casino and games like blackjack, craps, and video poker. I never gave much thought to playing casino poker.

I made my first trip to Atlantic City in the early '80s. Gambling was still fairly new to the East Coast. The Golden Nugget adorned the end of the boardwalk. The glitz and glamour of the casino and the mechanical birds in the gilded cage were a spectacle not seen before outside of Las Vegas. Located in the center of the boardwalk was the Playboy Club Casino. Many a young man's fancy of striking it rich at the tables gave way to a more lustful desire as he caught sight of the skimpily clad waitresses with the bunny tails. The Boardwalk was buzzing with the excitement of the casinos. I knew this was a place I wanted to visit as often as possible. I was enthralled with the whole scene. I was also totally clueless about the games and how the casinos operated.

My early trips to Atlantic City consisted of playing the slots. After several trips, I started to notice that the table game players were having a lot of fun and getting quite a bit of attention from the casino personnel. At that time there were no slot clubs, and only the table game players got comped. Bus trips to Atlantic City consisted of a five-hour ride to town with eight hours of gambling and a five hour ride back home. Since I was only playing slots, there were many trips when I ran out of money before the bus was due to take me back home. I started wandering around the casino looking at all the games. I wanted to try some of the games but was not sure how to go about it. Around that time my friend Rich started to tell me stories of his friend Andy.

Andy was a big gambler who was a "Rated Player" in Atlantic City. He had a system for roulette and always came back with hundreds and sometimes thousands of dollars. When my friend invited me to join him and Andy for a trip to Atlantic City, I jumped at the chance. I was finally going to see a real gambler in action at the tables. Our friend John also joined the group. We headed out one Sunday morning to stake our claim to the money the casinos would have to hand over once we stated using Andy's super roulette system. In the early days, the casinos in Atlantic City closed for a few hours at night. We arrived in Atlantic City and stopped at Harrah's in the Marina section away from the Boardwalk. We had time to eat breakfast before they opened the doors to the casino. While we ate we formulated our plan for making our big score.

Since Andy had his rating card, and it was his system, it was only logical that he would place the bets and work his magic. We all agreed to put up $20 each. This $80 bankroll was surely enough to get us started. After we turned it into a few hundred, we would take back our initial money and then proceed to run up the winnings until we reached a profit that was agreeable to all of us. We finished breakfast just as the door to the casino was opening up. We headed for the first roulette table.

After about 20 minutes of making bets, Andy turned to us and said we had hit a bad streak and were broke. He suggested we put up another $20 each to get us back on track. We forked over the money, which went the way of the first. We had been playing at the Marina and he suggested we head to the Boardwalk where we surely would have better luck. Again we each put up $20 and headed for Resorts on the Boardwalk. This time our money lasted about an hour. Finally, after going broke the third time I was asked to put up some more money to keep the partnership going. This was a turning point for me. I told the guys to count me out. They looked at me incredulously and asked "Why?"

I told them that I had just lost $60 on a game I knew nothing about without making a single bet. They shrugged and went back to the roulette table. I took a walk down the boardwalk of Atlantic City. During my walk I did a lot of thinking about what had just happened. I was foolish to waste money on a game I knew nothing about. I vowed that I would become an educated player and I promised myself that from that day forward I would never gamble a penny on any game or event unless I had researched it and I was in control of my own money. That was the day I started my casino education.

After a little research, I learned that roulette was one of the worst games to play in the casino. It had a high house edge of 5.26 percent. I chose to concentrate on other games. I started buying books and reading about the games and how the casinos operated. The first book I bought was *Beat the Dealer* by Edward O. Thorp. Today my library contains several hundred books on all the casino games and a variety of gambling related topics. I spent years studying how to play the casino games and how the casinos operated. I learned that blackjack, certain video poker games, and live poker are three games where a player can gain an edge.

When Foxwoods opened a short distance from my home in 1992, I was able to make more frequent trips to the casinos. I spent my time there playing blackjack. In 1994 I made my first visit to Las Vegas and immediately became a frequent visitor. It was in Las Vegas that I discovered the "full pay" video poker machines that offered over 100 percent payback when using proper strategy. These games kept me occupied and I never gave any thought to playing casino poker.

In May of 1998 I was hired as the Casino Gambling Guide for the Mining Company which later became About.com. The About network consists of over 500 Topic related sites neatly organized into many channels. The sites cover more than 50,000 subjects with over one million links to the best resources on the Internet. The About Casino Gambling site is dedicated to educating players about the casinos and the games. You will find hundreds of informative links, an interactive forum and free newsletter. I write weekly features to help readers get the most out of their casino visits.

The opportunities for skillful players are slowly dying out. The casinos do not like the players to have an edge in any game. For example, casinos are doing everything in their power to stop card counters. In Las Vegas they can bar players. In Atlantic City and other places where they can't bar players, they have taken different measures. They have multiple-deck games with lousy penetration, or they will choose to shuffle up on a player, or both. They can also restrict a player to flat betting a specified amount. Profitable video poker games are also starting to disappear. Many of the dollar games that offered over 100 percent payback are now being offered only on the quarter machines.

Apparently more players are coming to the same conclusion about the loss of the profitable games because I started to receive numerous requests from my readers for information about live poker. In order to answer their questions accurately, I decided it was time to learn how to play casino poker.

Chapter 3
The Journey Begins

I have tried every game on the main floor of the casino. When a new game comes along I at least give it a cursory try. Although I had played poker, I had never played in a casino poker room.

I had the misconception that casino poker was mostly no-limit games for professional players. This perception was bolstered by stories in the media about high stakes tournaments like the World Series of Poker in which players put up thousands of dollars just to enter. The truth is there are many low-limit games being played by average people every day in cardrooms around the country.

Poker is a game of skill. In the casino you are playing against the other players instead of the house. You will find all types of players in the cardroom. The skill levels of the players vary from the beginner just having fun to the skilled professional. By practicing and gaining experience some players win consistently.

I firmly believe that a player of average intelligence can learn to be successful playing in the casinos if he takes the time to educate himself about the casinos and the games. In my articles, I advocate that players take the time to learn all about the game they wish to play before venturing into the casino and risking any money at the tables.

Since I had never played casino poker, I thought this would be a good opportunity to practice what I preach. I planned to show that by using a disciplined approach I could be successful. I started to document the process that I used to learn how to play Texas

Hold'em. I had originally planned to write a few articles about the experience, sharing the knowledge that I learned, including my successes and mistakes, with my readers. After achieving success with playing Texas Hold'em it was suggested that I publish a detailed account of how I learned to play the game. This book is more than a text about how to play Texas Hold'em. It is also a journal of my journey from the kitchen to the cardroom

I was not sure which poker game I wanted to learn to play first, so I took a ride to the casino to check out the poker rooms. I live close to Foxwoods and the Mohegan Sun in Connecticut, so I had the opportunity to observe players in two poker rooms in the same afternoon. Both casinos offered two games for low limit player. Seven-card stud with $1–$5 limits and $3/$6 Texas Hold'em. I was familiar with seven-card stud but Texas Hold'em was completely foreign to me.

I took the time to talk with a few players of each game and I was given conflicting opinions about which game is better for new players to learn. As expected, each player thought his particular choice was the best. I decided to hold off choosing my game until I could gather some more information.

The Learning Tools

I am frequently asked if there is an easy way to learn how to play casino games like blackjack or video poker. Although learning to play correctly is not easy, there is a practical approach that will make the learning process enjoyable.

If you want to learn to play a casino game, I always recommend three essential tools to get you started. These will help form the foundation of your knowledge of the game. The three essentials are:

1. A book to teach you the basics and the rules of the game.
2. A tutorial software program that allows you to play, practice, and learn the game at home before risking money in the casino.
3. A video to show you how the game is played and to help reinforce what you learned in the book.

I knew I would use this approach to learn casino poker but I wasn't sure which game to learn first or which products were best to teach me what I needed to know. I wanted to get some expert advice. Since I was on my way to Las Vegas I contacted the Gambler's Book Shop to see if they could advise me. I met with General Manager Peter Ruchman and Marketing Director Howard Schwartz and discussed my project with them. Peter is an excellent poker player and advised me to learn how to play Texas Hold'em. He explained that it was more popular than stud and there were plenty of low-limit games available. I have played stud poker before, but since I have never played Hold'em I knew I was in for a real challenge. I asked Peter which products would be most helpful to a beginning player and he gave me his recommendations.

I picked up a book, two videotapes, and a software program. Now I had the tools I needed to start my poker education. I read the book on my flight back home and had a good grasp on the basics of the game.

There are two other things that you will need in your quest to learn casino games that cannot be purchased in a store. They are *patience* and *discipline*! These traits are important no matter which game you are trying to learn but they are vital to playing winning poker.

Part Two
The Basics

Chapter 4

Why Hold'em?

Coast to coast, from the Connecticut casinos to the cardrooms of California, Texas Hold'em is rapidly becoming the most popular poker game among low-limit players. There are several reasons for its popularity.

Texas Hold'em is fast-paced, and easy to learn. The game can be played with more players, which means bigger pots, making it very exciting and quite profitable for those players who make the effort to learn to play correctly.

The basic concepts of Hold'em are easy to learn and understand. Each player is dealt two personal cards and then five community cards are dealt face up in the middle of the table. Since there are five community cards you do not have to keep track of all the dead cards that were folded by your opponents as you do in stud. You can easily learn guidelines for which starting hands to play and which to fold.

Hold'em is a positional game. A dealer button rotates to the left after each hand. The player to the left of the dealer button acts first. You will always act in the same order for the entire hand. If you have the dealer button you will act last during each betting round. The later you act, the more information you will have to help decide whether you should enter the pot or fold your hand.

There are no antes. The player to the left of the dealer button puts up a blind bet usually equal to half of the minimum bet for the first round and the player to his left puts in a bet equal to the minimum bet. These are called the blinds. The rest of the players do not have to put any money in the pot unless they are calling the blind bet. This means that in a ten-handed game you will get to see eight hands for free. If you don't have a playable starting hand you can toss it in and wait for your next hand.

Hold'em is a faster game than seven-card stud. You can play a hand in about two minutes. This means you will see more hands during your playing session. This allows you to be more selective which should lead to profitability if you capitalize on the poor play of your opponents.

The use of five community cards, called "board" cards, means that more players can play. A full game will have ten, or sometimes, 11 players. Since many players will enter a hand, there is a potential for bigger pots in Hold'em. There are a wide variety of hands that can be made from the five community cards and the player's two pocket cards. All of the players are using 71 percent of the same cards to make their hands. This means that there is no way to immediately determine who has the biggest hand. When you are playing stud, if you saw that your opponent had two Aces showing, you could determine if he had you beat and then fold. Since this is not the case in Texas Hold'em, more players will stay in the hand longer, adding to the total size of the pot.

In a low-limit $3/$6 game, there could be $30 in the pot before the first community cards are revealed. It is not uncommon to see pots in the $50–$100 ranges. In this game, if there were five players entering the pot and staying to the end, making minimum bets with no raising, the pot would be $90. You can afford to be selective in your starting hands because it is possible that winning one hand can cover the cost of your blind bets for the entire evening.

You always know how the strength of your hand stacks up against the best possible hand during each betting round. A pair of Aces is the best two-card starting hand. This changes once the first three community cards are flopped and again when the fourth and then the fifth cards are turned over. You can tell the best possible hand by looking at the board cards. Although it is not certain that one of your opponents will actually have the best hand, you can assess the strength of your hand in relation to the best theoretical hand and determine if you have a chance of winning the pot. This is known as reading the board and will be discussed in detail later in this book.

Limit Texas Hold'em, which is the game being described in this book, has fixed betting limits for each round. Most cardrooms offer several Hold'em games at different betting limits, so you can choose a game that is within the limits of your bankroll.

The most compelling reason to play Texas Hold'em is that you are choosing a game that can be profitable for a player who takes the time to learn how to make the correct decisions.

Chapter 5

How to Play Texas Hold'em

The rules of the game are fairly easy to learn. Limit Hold'em has structured betting, and the lowest limit you will find in most casinos is a $2/$4 or $3/$6 game. Other limits you may find are $5/$10 or $10/$20 or higher. I will be using the $3/$6 game as an example in this book. That means the minimum bet is $3 during the first two rounds of betting and the minimum bet is $6 during the last two betting rounds. These same limits are used when you raise as well.

The Dealer

Since the casino supplies a dealer, one player must be the "designated" dealer who will act last during the betting rounds. A disk or "button" is used to identify the dealer and this is rotated to the left after each hand. Unlike stud, all the players do not ante each round. Blind bets are posted to generate a starting pot.

The Start

To start a new hand two "blind" bets are put up or "posted." The player immediately to the left of the player with the dealer button puts up or "posts" the *small blind* which is approximately half the minimum bet. Since there are no 50¢ chips, the small blind for the

$3/$6 game is one dollar. The player to the left of the small blind posts the *big blind* which is equal to the minimum bet which is $3 for this game. The rest of the players do not put up any money to start the hand. Because the button rotates around the table, each player will eventually act as the big blind, small blind and dealer. It will cost you $4 every time the deal makes a complete rotation around the table.

The Opening

After the blinds are posted each player is dealt two cards face down, with the player on the small blind receiving the first card and the player with the dealer button getting the last card. The first betting round begins with the player to the left of the big blind either putting in $3 to "call" the blind bet, or putting in $6 to "raise" the big blind or folding his hand. The betting goes around the table in order until it reaches the player who posted the small blind. That player can call the bet by putting in $2 since a dollar bet was already posted. The last person to act is the big blind. If no one has raised, the dealer will ask if they would like the option. This means the big blind has the option to raise or just "check."

By checking the player does not put in any more money. A rookie mistake sometimes occurs here. Because the blind is a live bet, the player with the big blind has already put his bet in. I have seen some players throw their cards in not realizing that they are already in the hand. Another rookie mistake is betting or folding your cards when it is not your turn. You must wait your turn before you act.

The Flop

After the first betting round is completed the dealer will "burn" or discard the top card on the deck. This is done to make sure no one could have accidentally seen the top card. Three cards are dealt and turned face up in the middle of the table. This is known as the "flop." These are community cards used by all the players. Another betting round begins with the first active player to the left of the dealer button. The minimum bet for this round is also $3.

The Turn

When the betting round after the flop is completed, the dealer burns another card and turns a fourth card face up in the middle of the table. This is referred to as the "turn." The minimum bet after the turn is now $6 and begins again with the first active player to the left of the button.

The River

Following the betting round for the turn, the dealer will burn another card and turn a fifth and final card face up. This is called the "river," and the final betting round begins with $6 being the minimum bet. There is usually a three or four raise maximum during all betting rounds except if the play becomes heads up with two players. Then the raises are unlimited.

The Showdown

To determine the winner, the players may use any combination of their two hole cards (either one, or both) and the five cards on the "Board" to form the highest five-card hand. In some rare cases the best hand will be the five cards on board. In that case the active players will split the pot. A sixth card is never used to break a tie.

I was playing in a game with a player who was obviously a novice. He was in the hand with one other player. At the showdown the board cards were Kh-Kc-9s-9c-Ah. There were two pairs on board with an Ace. The first player turned over a Jack and Queen. The new player turned over his pocket cards to reveal a pair of deuces. At which point he proudly exclaimed that he had "Three pairs!" He was upset when the dealer explained to him that only five cards played and it was a split pot. This is a good example of why you should know the rules of a game before sitting down to play in the casino.

Additional Information

The five community cards are referred to as the "board." Unlike seven-card stud, all the players use the same cards. Because of this you don't have to remember cards that were folded by other players.

Although the game looks deceptively simple, there is a lot of strategy involved. Your position in relation to the dealer button is important in deciding which beginning hands you play. It is also important to learn how to read the board to determine the best possible hand.

In elementary school they teach you that you must learn the three **R**s:

Reading, **R**iting, and **R**ithmatic

In Texas Hold'em you must learn the three **P**s:

Position, **P**ower, and **P**atience

You need to be aware of your position when deciding which starting hands to play. You want to play powerful starting hands for that position and you need the patience to wait for these hands. These will all be covered in the following chapters. The next page shows a visual representation of the game.

Chapter 6
Texas Hold'em

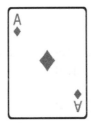

Your starting cards are called pocket or hole cards.
First Betting Round

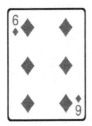

The first three community cards are called the flop.
Second Betting Round

The fourth community card is called the turn.

Third Betting Round

The fifth community card is called the river.

Final Betting Round

Chapter 7

Hierarchy of Poker Hands

Royal Flush
This is the best poker hand: Ten (T), Jack (J), Queen (Q), King (K), and Ace (A) of the same suit.

Straight Flush
Five cards, all of the same suit that are in sequence.

Four-of-a-Kind
Four cards of equal rank: Qc, Qh, Qd, Qs.

Full House
Three cards of equal rank, and two other cards of the equal rank (three of a kind and a pair): T T T 5 5.

Flush.
Any five cards of the same suit: As, Ts, 9s, 7s, 5s.

Straight
Five cards of mixed suits, in sequence.

Three-of-a-Kind
Any three cards of equal rank.

Two Pair
Two cards of equal rank and two other cards of equal rank.

One Pair
Two cards of equal rank.

Chapter 8
Who's Got the Button?

Before I started studying Texas Hold'em and learning how to play properly, I thought all I had to do was learn the starting hands and what to do after the flop. I knew absolutely nothing about one of the most vital aspects of the game, position. Position ranks second only to starting cards in deciding whether or not to play your hand. Understanding position is an important concept if you want to be a winning player.

Your position is determined by where you are sitting in relation to the dealer's button. Unlike games like stud, where the betting order changes with each betting round, the order is fixed in Texas Hold'em. Before the flop the person to the left of the big blind bets first. After the flop the first active player to the left of the dealer button acts first. If you are in early position you will remain there for all betting rounds.

If you play a weak or marginal hand in early position before the flop, you are at risk of getting raised by those acting after you. There is also a possibility of multiple raises. If you decide to fold, you have cost yourself a bet without ever seeing any other cards. Before you make a bet in early position you have to ask yourself if the hand is strong enough to call a raise from a player in a later position. If you would not call a raise with your starting hand you should throw it away. Some hands are drawing hands that play better with many opponents calling the pot. If you have to act first, you have no idea how many players will call or fold.

When you are in the late position you will have an idea of the strength of you opponents' hands by how they bet. If there have been no raises you can play weaker starting hands and hope that the flop will fit your hand. If there have been no callers, and you are last to act, you can sometimes steal the blind merely by raising with a marginal hand because of your position. You will hear players refer to this play as a positional raise. In late position after the flop, you have more information to help you decide how to play. You can raise if your opponents bet or you can bet if everyone has checked. You may decide to check to gain a free card. If there have been bets or raises before you, and your hand was not helped by the flop, you can fold without it costing you an additional bet.

In early position you do not have this luxury after the flop. If you bet there is the chance that you will be raised. If you check in the hopes of check raising, there is a chance that everyone else will check and you will lose some potential money that would have gone into the pot.

The chart below shows a quick reference to the positions in a ten-person game. If there were fewer players in the game you would adjust this.

Table Position in a Ten Player Game

1. Small Blind   Early Position. Under the Gun after the flop.
2. Big Blind   Early Position. Has the option of checking on first round before the flop.
3. Under the Gun   Early Position. Acts first before the flop.
4. Early   Second person to act before the flop.
5. Early/Middle   Third person to act before the flop. Middle after the flop.
6. Middle   Can play a few more starting hands if no raises.
7. Middle   Can play a few more starting hands if no raises.
8. Middle/Late   May be considered middle in aggressive game.
9. Late   Second to last after the flop.
10. Dealer   "On the Button" acts last after the flop.

The person "On the Button" gets to act last, except for the first betting round, which starts with the first player to the left of the big blind. A player acting first is referred to as being "under the gun." After the flop, the player posting the small blind is under the gun if they are still in the hand. The dealer button rotates after each hand so your position changes after each hand is completed.

As a player it is important to be conscious of your position for each hand. I have found it beneficial to mentally note my position before the cards are dealt. By repeating my position to myself, I am able to quickly determine whether or not to play a hand when I glance at my pocket cards.

There are only about 20 hands that are strong enough to play from an early position. Players are making a big mistake if they play weak or marginal hands without giving consideration to their position.

Chapter 9

Starting Hands

The most important decision a player will make in Texas Hold'em is which starting hands to play. Most players lose because they play too many hands. There are 169 possible two-card starting hands. Hands of equal rank but different suits are counted as one because they have the same value before the flop. For instance an Ace and King of hearts has the same value as the Ace and King of spades, clubs, or diamonds. Out of these 169 hands there are only about 75 that are playable. Which of these 75 you play will be determined by your position to the dealer button. Not all of these hands can be played from every position. Cards of the same suit are more powerful than unsuited cards because of their flush potential. Strong starting hands such as big pairs have a better chance of holding up to make the winning hand than smaller cards.

The combination of starting hands will fall into four categories. Actually you could further simplify this by noting that there are two categories. Big card hands that will win in a small field without improvement and drawing hands that need help

Pocket Pairs

Big pairs are powerful starting hands. A pair of Aces is the best starting hand but a pair of deuces is a weak hand that can only be played in late position in an unraised pot. Some medium pairs can win the pot, but with the smaller pairs you will be looking to make a set or possibly a straight draw.

Connectors

Cards that are next to each other are called connectors. They can be suited or unsuited. These are hands like K-Q, J-T, or 9-8. Connectors are used in making straights. Suited connectors can make straight flushes, straights, or flushes.

Gapped Cards

Gappers are cards that have one or more gaps between them. These are hands such as Q-T, J-9, or T-8. The smaller the gap the easier it is to make a straight. With a hand that has a gap you are looking to fill the gap for a straight or a straight draw. As with the connectors, the suited cards have more potential of making a flush or straight flush.

Big Cards

Cards of higher value than ten are considered big cards. Suited cards are more valuable than unsuited cards. These hands still fall into the categories of connectors or gapped hands; however, because of their higher value they can sometimes stand on their own if you pair them up on the flop. You should tighten your starting requirements if your cards are not suited and there are a lot of players in the pot. Big cards play better against fewer players.

A pair of Aces is the strongest starting hand before the flop. With only two cards there is nothing higher. Aces do not always stand up as the winning hand after the flop. The weakest starting hand is an unsuited seven and deuce. There are five gaps between the two cards making a straight impossible. Because they are not suited you cannot make a flush either.

Many players in low-limit games will play any Ace regardless of the second card. These players have found themselves a loser when an Ace flops and they are beat out by a player with a bigger kicker. A kicker is an unpaired card in your hand that will determine the winner in the event of a tie. Example: If the winning hand was a pair of Aces and you held A-K and your opponent held A-J, your King would beat his Jack. In this example the King and Jack are the kickers. Some players will just play any two cards. They are looking for miracle flops to improve their hands. Although it is possible to get a miracle flop, more often than not you won't get it. To be a consistent winner a player needs to learn the correct starting hands.

The Hold'em Arrow

David Sklansky was the first to publish a table of the starting hands in his book *Hold'em Poker* in 1976. The table ranks the starting hands and an explanation is given as to the proper position from which to play them. This list of starting hands has become more or less the standard for knowledgeable players. There are some hands that will be played differently depending on the number of players, the type of the game and whether or not the pot was raised before your turn to act. A player will need to tighten up or loosen these guidelines accordingly.

As I studied the table of starting hands I thought a graphic representation would be easier to understand. I started to draw out some ideas on graph paper. I wanted a design that would help me understand the hands in relation to the dealer button.

I found I was not the only one who thought a chart was easier to help beginners understand the starting hands. In *Hold'em Excellence*, Lou Krieger had a "Start Chart" which consists of two vertical charts of the starting hands. One was for suited and the other was for unsuited hands. His charts were helpful but I still was looking for another way to relate to the hands.

I continued drawing out different configurations of the starting hands. I finally thought of a linear design. I drew a dealer button on the right side of the sheet. I then started drawing the pairs on the line next to the button. Since the player to the left of the dealer acts first, I put the pair of Aces to the immediate left with the rest of the pairs in descending order with the deuces being the farthest hand on the dealer's left side. The hands closest to the dealer's left would be the early position hands. Since the poker table is circular, as you get closer to the right side of the dealer button you would be in later position. These would be the hands toward the left side of the sheet.

I proceeded to fill in the other starting hands. I placed the suited cards on the top of the line of pairs and placed the unsuited hands underneath. When I finished I noticed that the chart looked like an arrow. It also showed how the number of starting hands increased in the later positions. I found this chart helped me visualize the hands in the order I was looking for. I color-coded the hands for early, middle, and late positions.

Visualizing the chart I could adjust the hands on the border of each position depending on the type of game. These positions are not written in stone and can be adjusted for the type of game I am playing in. For example, in a very loose, passive game I might consider playing the pair of 9s or 8s in early position instead of the middle position. In an aggressive game, the suited Queen-Ten may move to middle position.

Suited

Unsuited

DEAL

	AA	
AK	KK	AK
KQ AQ	QQ	AQ KQ
QJ KJ AJ	JJ	AJ KJ QJ
JT QT KT AT	TT	AT KT QT JT
T9 J9 Q9 K9 A9	99	A9 K9 Q9 J9 T9
98 T8 J8 Q8 K8 A8	88	A8 J8 T8 98
87 97 T7 K7 A7	77	A7
76 86 96 K6 A6	66	
65 75 K5 A5	55	
54 K4 A4	44	
K3 A3	33	
K2 A2	22	

EARLY
MIDDLE
LATE

37

Chapter 10

Any Ace Won't Do

We often use the expression, "That's my Ace in the hole," when referring to a contingency plan or a good backup to help get us out of a jam if things don't go the way we anticipated. This is an expression derived from poker games such as five-card stud, where a single Ace in the hole could be a valuable card to possess.

In Texas Hold'em, however, a single Ace is not as powerful as some players would like to think. Many Hold'em players think they found the "Holy Grail" when they look at their starting hand and see a single Ace in the hole.

Everyone loves to see Aces in their starting hands. How often will you get one? You will be dealt at least one Ace about 15 percent of the time before the flop. Which means that 85 percent of the time you won't have an Ace. Maybe that is the reason that players get so excited when they see an Ace. The chances of one of your opponents holding an Ace at the same time you do is directly related to the number of players in the game with you. This chart shows the Absence of Aces before the flop based on the number of players. The figures in the chart are expressed in percent.

# of Players	Probability that no player has an Ace (including yourself)	If you have an Ace the probability that no other player has an Ace	If you have no Ace, the probability that no other player has an Ace
2	71.87	88.24	84.49
3	60.28	77.45	70.86
4	50.14	67.57	58.95
5	41.34	58.57	48.60
6	33.76	50.41	39.68
7	27.27	43.04	32.05
8	21.76	36.43	25.58
9	17.13	30.53	20.14
10	13.28	25.31	15.61

If you are playing at a full table with ten players and hold a single Ace the probability that there is no other player also holding an Ace is 25.31 percent. That means that when you have an Ace one of the nine other players will have an Ace 75 percent of the time. This is why you need to consider your other card, known as your kicker, to go with that single Ace.

Playing an Ace with a small kicker is referred to as playing a "weak Ace." When you do this, you are setting yourself up to be beaten by a player who holds an Ace with a higher kicker. If you hold:

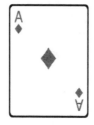 

And the flop is

If one of your opponents holds an Ace your chance of winning with your 5 as a kicker is very slim. Your opponent would have to hold a 4, 3, or deuce in order for you to win. There are only 12 cards that he could hold that would make you a winner and along with three other fives that would make a tie. If your opponent held any other card, you would be beaten if it went to the river with no improvements to either hand.

You also have to consider that you may pair your kicker instead of the Ace. In the above example, if you paired your five, you would have a small pair with an Ace. If, however, you play your single Ace with a bigger card there will be situations where you would almost rather pair your kicker than your Ace. If you hold

and the flop is

You now have the top pair with the best kicker. Anyone else holding Queen is sure to give you action with this flop. You might also get action from players holding the single Ace who are looking for an Ace to appear on the turn or river. If this happens you will still have them beat with two pairs.

If you are in a game and notice that many of the players are playing a single Ace then you have the opportunity to make some money from them if you only play your Ace with a strong kicker. Many players will refuse to fold a pair of Aces even if they have a weak kicker. These players will call you all the way to the river only to be beaten by your strong kicker.

When there are five or more players in the hand, a pair of Aces will only hold up about 35 percent of the time. A single Ace will win even less often but, still, many players will stay in the hand with a single Ace and call all the way to the river. If you want to be a winning player, you will avoid playing an unsuited weak Ace from any position. In late position, in an unraised pot, you can play a suited Ace because of its flush potential.

Chapter 11

Any Suited

Some players in low-limit games will play any two suited cards from any position. They are looking only for a flush. It doesn't matter to them if the cards have too many gaps to form a straight and no potential to win if they make a pair. I have seen players call the pot from early position with a hand like:

Being dealt two suited cards as a starting hand is a fairly common occurrence. The probability of being dealt this hand is about 23.5 percent. This means there will be a lot of opportunities for those players who will play a hand containing any two suited cards. Making a flush with this hand, however, is a lot more difficult than most players realize.

When you start with two suited cards you will flop two or more of that suit only about 11 percent of the time. That means you are an 8-to-1 underdog before the flop. You will flop a complete flush only 0.84 percent of the time. The odds are 118-to-1 against this happening. If you start suited, and stay through the river card, you will make a flush about 5.77 percent of the time. That means that about 94 percent of the time you start suited, you will not make your flush if you stay to the river card. This type of hand will cost you a lot of money if you consistently play it without regard to the value of the suited cards.

For example, assume you are playing in a $3/$6 game where the pot is never raised. It will cost you $3 each for the pre-flop and flop, and $6 on the turn for a total of $12 to see the river card. You play this hand 100 times. You will win six times and lose 94 times. It will cost you $1,128 to play this hand 94 times. To break even you would have to win an average of $188 each of the six times that you did win.

This is an overly simplistic example because there are plenty of other hands that could be made from two starting cards. Also, most players would fold if they only flopped one card to their suited starting cards. I just want to point out that because your two starting cards are suited doesn't necessarily mean that you should play this type of hand all the time.

Many players lose with this type of hand and then try to justify playing it by pointing out that the cards were suited. In reality, just being suited is the wrong reason to play these types of hands. Sometimes other players will beat you when they do make the occasional flush with this type of hand. If this happens don't get upset, because you can be confident that you will win more money from this type of player in the long run.

Chapter 12
Early Position

I can't stress enough the fact that Hold'em is a *positional* game. When you are in early position you need a strong hand to enter the pot. You have no idea what the players who follow you will do. It is extremely costly to enter the pot with marginal cards only to be raised or re-raised. This is where the category of big cards definitely comes into play but not all big cards can be played in early position. When you are in early position, you want to play a hand that can hopefully stand up to a raise. This is especially true if you are "under the gun," the first player to act.

When I am under the gun, I will limit my play to big pairs or an Ace with a Jack or higher. In a very passive game, I may loosen up just a bit, but it is usually better to play tight when you are under the gun. Here are some of the other hands playable from early or any position.

Aces

Pocket Rockets, Bullets, American Airlines, no matter what you call them a pair of Aces by any other name is still the best starting hand you can have. If this were two-card showdown, you would be a winner every time. But this is Hold'em and you still have a ways to go before you rake in the chips. With Aces, your hand will hold up against one or two players most of the time but will win about 35 percent of the time with five or more players in the pot. Getting your pair of Aces beaten is known as getting your Aces "cracked." It happens and is a fact of the game. Because of this, you want to thin the field if possible but you also want to get as much money in the pot for the times that your hand does win.

It's okay to raise from any position with Aces. When you raise from early position you will have a good shot at thinning the field. Players with marginal drawing hands will probably fold. But there are some considerations on how to maximize the money in the pot without giving your opponents the proper odds to draw out on you. Most players will not fold their hand to a raise once they have entered the pot. In middle position you want to raise to drive out any of the players acting after you who might hold marginal hands while getting more money from those already in the pot. If the pot has already been raised when it gets to you, go ahead and reraise. It's okay to cap the betting if you get re-raised again. Most of the time you will raise with Aces, but sometimes you may want to mix up your style of play.

In late position, if most of the players have entered the pot, you may want to just call when you are in the blinds with a pair of Aces. When you raise from the blind you are letting everyone know that you have a strong hand. Sometimes, you may be better off using a little deception. By not raising you can see the flop and, either bet if the field is large or try for a check raise if you are heads ups with a single aggressive player. You do not want to slow play a pair of aces that gets no help on the flop against a large number of players.

After the flop you must look at the board carefully. If the flop brings all little cards, your Aces may still be the best hand. If there has been a lot of action before the flop and the flop brings a King or two or more face cards, you might have a problem. If one of your opponents was raising with a pair of Kings they now have a set. If they were holding two face cards they could have flopped two pairs. If you bet and are raised, you will have to proceed with caution.

Kings

When I first started playing Hold'em, I heard some players refer to "Paint" cards and had no idea what they were talking about. I soon found out that paint cards were the cards that I used to call picture cards, because they had a picture of the King, Queen, or Jack. I suppose they do resemble paintings more than they do pictures. Anyway the King is the big paint card and when you start with a pair of them you have the second best starting hand. Only a pair of Aces can beat you at this point. The probability of being dealt any pair is 220 to 1 (0.45 percent) or less than one-half of a percent, so the chances of one of your opponents holding a pair of Aces when you are dealt a pair of Kings is slim but it does happen. However, the probability of a player holding a single Ace before the flop is about 15 percent. If an Ace appears in the flop you could lose out to a player who will play any Ace. Because of this you want to play the Kings as aggressively as possible to narrow the field.

It is advisable to raise with Kings from any position. If the pot has been raised go ahead and reraise. Cap the betting if you can. If no Ace appears on the flop go ahead and raise again if a player bets before you. You want to make it very expensive for anyone holding a single Ace to stay in the pot. When I first started playing Hold'em, I would try to get fancy and slow play my Kings in hopes of maybe raising on the turn or river, when the betting limit went up. Quite a few times this backfired on me when an Ace would show up on the turn or the river. After losing to players holding hands like A-6 off suit I decided not to slow play my Kings. I later learned that you should never slow play a single pair as they are too vulnerable in a multiway pot.

If an Ace should flop or two high cards, such as J-10 or higher, you could be in trouble if someone raises. If there is a raise when an Ace flops it's more than likely that someone was playing a single Ace. Because it is correct strategy to play high cards in your starting hands, a flop containing two or three high cards may give your opponent two pairs, a straight or a straight draw. You shouldn't automatically fold when there is betting, but you do need to reassess the situation if there is raising going on. Many players, myself included, have been guilty of getting married to a pair of Kings or other high pairs when the flop brings two or more high cards. The reasoning is that it is possible to draw another King on the turn or river. This may hold up against two pairs but you might find that you are drawing dead against a straight. Because being dealt a pair of Kings doesn't happen that often, it's natural to want to play them to the end.

However, there are times when you just have to let it go and fold the big guys. A winning player is one who can do this.

Queens and Jacks

Queens and Jacks are the "Baby Paint" cards. Obviously Queens are a little stronger than Jacks, but both of these are vulnerable to the single Aces and Kings that many low-limit players will play, if an overcard shows up on the flop. (An overcard is any card higher than the ones you hold.) Normally I will just call with these pairs, unless the game is extremely tight and I think that a lot of players will fold, thus thinning the field. If the game is tight I will even raise under the gun, but if I get re-raised I know I'm in trouble. You will have to pay attention to your opponents. I have probably saved more money by not raising pre-flop with these hands in most low-limit games.

If you see an overcard on the flop you shouldn't hesitate to bet the hand, but be wary if there is a raise. If no card higher than your Queen or Jack appears on the flop you should raise with the top pair if a player ahead of you bets. You want to make it expensive for anyone who might be holding a single Ace or King. If you should happen to flop a set of Queens or Jacks, then you might want to just call if there is a bet and then go for a raise on the turn when the betting limits are higher. The problem with starting with a pair is that you usually need to flop a set or a straight or straight draw to improve your hand, as you are vulnerable if there are overcards on the flop.

Tens

Tens are actually the start of the medium pairs. Since most players will play any face cards they can easily be beaten if any overcards appear on the flop. Pocket tens can be played in early position in loose, passive games, but you might want to pass if the game is very aggressive. Since all straights require the use of a ten or a five, holding tens does have an advantage if the flop brings cards that may need a ten to complete a straight draw. Since you have two of them, it is unlikely that another player will have the other ones. If the flop brings all low cards, making your tens top pair, you should raise if anyone bets before you after the flop. You need to make it expensive for anyone holding overcards to stay in the pot. If the flop contains Aces or faces, you will probably be best to fold your tens if you have no other outs such as a straight draw.

Ace-King

The combination of Ace-King is sometimes referred to as "Big Slick." Years ago it was called Santa Barbara after an oil spill of the coast of California. When there was the big oil spill off the coast of Alaska, players were quick to note that AK is also the abbreviation for that state, making it even more appropriate. Regardless of why it is called this, I can tell you from what I have seen that the way some players play this hand is anything but "slick." Most experts agree that A-K, either suited or unsuited, is one of the most misplayed hands in limit Hold'em. An Ace and a King are two of the best cards you can hold when they are paired, but when you have a single of each you have a drawing hand. Many players will play A-K as though they were holding a pair of Aces or Kings. You usually need to improve this hand to give it any value. If you do pair one of your cards on the flop, you will have top pair and top kicker. You will flop and Ace or a King about 30 percent of the time. Many people look at that statistic and think it's a high percentage, but look at the other side and you will realize that you won't flop either an Ace or King 70 percent of the time. This figure is the same for any two unpaired cards you hold before the flop.

In early position, you should raise with A-K suited and call with an unsuited combination. The suited cards will give you the potential of having the nut flush if you make a flush. If you feel that raising will limit the field, then you can raise with A-K unsuited as well. If the pot is raised ahead of you, re-raise with A-K suited and with A-K if you think it will limit the field.

If the flop does not help you out and there is a bet and a raise, your two overcards will not have much value. I have seen players play Ace-King all the way to the river when there is betting and raising going on. If there are several players in the hand betting and raising, you are probably going to be drawing dead if you do pair your Ace or King especially if the board cards show the possibility of a straight or flush. Players who refuse to abandon A-K, and play it to the end in hopes a catching a pair on the river, lose more money by doing so.

Ace-Queen or Ace-Jack

An Ace with a Queen, or Jack, is a playable hand from early position. You have a strong kicker if there is an Ace on the flop or you have a big pair with the best kicker if a Queen or a Jack should flop. When these cards are suited you will have the added potential for making a flush. If, however, the pot is raised ahead of you, and you have an unsuited Ace-Jack, you may be in for trouble as a player raising from early position may have a big pair. You have to consider who is doing the raising.

Ace-Ten

In blackjack, Ace-Ten is the best hand but in Texas Hold'em it's not as strong as some players would like to believe. From early position an A-T suited is playable, but the unsuited A-T is a middle position hand. Although a Ten is considered a big card it is not extremely powerful, as many players will be holding face cards.

Big Connectors and Gappers

From early position, a hand of K-Q is the only other unsuited connector to play. You can play suited connectors K-Qs, Q-Js, and J-Ts. You can also play suited gappers K-Js, K-Ts, and Q-Ts. With these hands you can flop the nut straight or a large flush. If the pot has been raised, you would be best to forgo these smaller gapped hands. (In this book a small letter "s" next to a pair of cards, signifies that they are the same suit.)

　　　　Remember when you are in early position and the player under the gun, or another player, raises it usually means that they have a powerful hand. If the raise comes from a solid player it would be best to err on the side of caution and throw away some of the lower hands. Just because a hand is considered playable from early position, it does not mean you will play it in all types of games. A hand that you would play in a loose passive game may be unplayable in a tight aggressive game.

Here is a quick reference for early position.

Raise

Raise and reraise with a pair of Aces and Kings and with A-K suited. If you are in a tight game, and think it will narrow the field, or you are the first to act in late position, you can raise with A-K and also a pair of Queens or Jacks.

Hand	Call-Raise	If Raised
A-A	Raise	Reraise
K-K	Raise	Reraise
A-Ks	Raise	Reraise
Q-Q	Raise—narrow field/late	Call
J-J	Raise—narrow field/late	Call
T-T	Call	Call
A-Q	Call	Call
A-Js	Call	Call
A-Ts	Call	Call
K-Qs	Call	Call
K-Js	Call	Call
K-Ts	Call	Call
Q-Ts	Call	Call
Q-Js	Call	Call
J-Ts	Call	Call
A-K	Raise—narrow field/late	Call
A-Q	Call	Call
A-J	Call	Call
K-Q	Call	Call

"*s*" denotes that the cards are suited.

Fold

Everything else.

Chapter 13
Middle Position

In middle position you can obviously play all the early position hands. The additional hands that are playable in middle position are drawing hands. They are not likely to win a pot without some sort of improvement. You also can play a few more hands because you will have more information about your situation. If a player in early position raised, you know there is a potentially strong hand in front of you, and you will need to tighten up your starting requirements. If there has been a re-raise you may want to bail out altogether. In middle position you can also start to judge how many players will be active in the hand. If everyone has called when it gets to you, then you know you will have a multiway pot. In a ten-handed game, middle position is the player in the 5, 6, and 7 seat after the dealer button. Players 1 and 2 are the blinds, so if you are the number 5 player there are only two players acting before you before the flop. If there is a raise in front of you, it will usually mean you are up against a big hand.

Anytime you call from middle position, you are adding to the pot odds, making it appropriate for callers with weaker hands to enter the pot. Calling a raise will add additional money to the pot and may entice even more players to enter because of the size of the pot. You will be getting better pot odds but you will be up against more players, decreasing your chances of winning.

Medium Pairs

Pocket 9s, 8s, and 7s are considered medium pairs. They are not the strongest pairs you can start with and they require you to play them a little selectively. You have to be extremely careful when the flop brings overcards.

You will usually need to improve these pairs on the flop to have them hold up. When you start with a medium or small pocket pair, your chance for improving is a little more limited. You will need to flop a set in most cases for a winning hand. If the pot has been raised before it is your turn to act, you should probably pass on these medium pairs.

I tend to play conservatively before the flop and will fold this hand if it is raised. If you routinely play this hand, calling two or more bets, then you will lose more in the long run. With these pairs if you don't flop a set or straight draw, you will have to release them if the flop contains overcards and there is a bet. One or more overcards will flop more than 90 percent of the time.

Suited Ace

Ace with a suited nine, eight or seven can be added to your starting hands in this position. You are looking to make the nut flush or are hoping for Aces up. If there is an Ace on the flop and you get action, you might find yourself up against a higher kicker. You don't want to play this hand heads up against a player who has raised. You are not getting proper odds for your flush draw and you will end losing more in the long run.

Big Cards

Unsuited big cards, Tens through Kings join the list of middle-position hands. Although these are big cards, if you play them against a few players and flop one pair, you may find yourself up against a higher pair with a weak kicker. These are drawing hands. If there are a lot of players calling in front of you, some of these hands can turn into trouble hands. If the flop contains all big cards, then you must be careful. You would like to flop a straight or a straight draw that utilizes your two pocket cards. If you make two pairs on the flop, you still should be aware of the possibility that someone else may have made a straight because other players may also be holding big cards. If you hold:

and the flop is

you have two pairs. If you are first to act and are raised, you could be up against a pair of Aces. You should raise the pot. If you are re-raised you must use caution. You are a loser if your opponent holds:

Play these big cards in an unraised multiway pot. If you do flop top pair, go ahead and bet. If you get raised you may have to abandon the hand.

Suited Connectors and Gappers
K-9s, Q-9s, T-9s, 9-8s, J-9s

These are all drawing hands that you want to play in an unraised pot with many players. They are marginal hands that will require you to hit a big flop to continue. I will play these in late middle position only if there are at least four players in the hand. If there is a wild player to my left who has been raising it up, I will usually pass on these hands. T-9s and 9-8s are connectors that you would almost rather make a straight with than a baby flush. K-9s and Q-9s have the possibility of making a big flush. When you make a flush, the Ace of your suit will appear on the flop about a third of the time. If the Ace does not appear, and you are raised, you have to be aware that you may be up against the nut flush.

Here is a quick reference for middle position.

Hand	Call—# Players	If Raised
9-9	Call	Call 4 or more
8-8	Call	Call 4 or more
7-7	Call	Call 4 or more
A-9s	Call 4 or more	Fold
A-8s	Call 4 or more	Fold
A-7s	Call 4 or more	Fold
K-9s	Call 4 or more	Fold
Q-9s	Call 4 or more	Fold
J-9s	Call 4 or more	Fold
T-9s	Call 4 or more	Fold
9-8s	Call 4 or more	Fold
A-T	Call	Fold
K-J	Call 4 or more	Fold
K-T	Call 4 or more	Fold
Q-J	Call 4 or more	Fold
Q-T	Call 4 or more	Fold
J-T	Call 4 or more	Fold

"s" denotes that the cards are suited.

Chapter 14

Late Position

When you are in late position, or last to act, you have a big advantage. You will have the best position for all four betting rounds. You will have more information about your opponents because they have to act before you do. You can determine the strength of their hands and be able to evaluate how many players you will be up against. You can also enter the pot with weaker starting hands if there have been no raises before it is your turn to act. If you are first to enter the pot, you can sometimes raise with hands that you normally would call with in early position. Late position is the time to raise with Queens and Jacks and unsuited A-K or A-Q if no one else has called the pot. Remember this is done to further limit the field or even win the blinds. If there are callers ahead of you, it will not drive any of them out. In low limit games, once a player enters the pot he will usually call raises to see the flop.

If you find yourself in an unraised pot with many players, you can play the weaker suited connectors very cheaply. In late position there is less of a chance that a player acting after you will raise you. If you hit a flop and make a straight, you will have a good chance of scooping a large pot. If you don't, it has only cost you a single bet. If you must cold call a raise or two, you can easily bail out when you are in late position and save yourself money.

When you are the dealer you are "on the Button" and last to act before the blinds. If you have a playable hand, and no one else has entered the pot, you may be able to steal the blinds with a raise if you don't think the players will defend their blinds. This should not be tried if you have a trash hand. Many players will play any hand on the button. This is a costly mistake. Being last to act does not make your hand any stronger. It just means that you can enter the pot cheaper because the blinds will usually not raise unless they have a big hand. You should be extremely cautious if you are raised from a player in the blinds. This is a sure indication that they have a strong hand.

Small Pairs

Play any pair in an unraised pot with at least five callers. If you hold a pair you will flop a set about 11.76 percent of the time. This means the odds are 7.5-to-1 against you. With five callers you are getting close to proper odds. If you flop a set, you will have a big hand and have the advantage of acting late in the round. If there are six or more players in the hand, you can call one raise. Don't cold call two raises with a small pair, and be careful if the raise came from an early position player. With less than six players, fold if raised in front.

Ace Any
A-6s, A-2s and A-9, A-8, A-7

You can play any suited Ace in late position with enough callers. If you flop a flush, you will have the nut flush or you may flop a nut flush draw. You will only make a flush about six percent of the time, which means that these hands can be trouble. As with the middle position suited-Ace hands, you can be in trouble if an Ace appears on the flop, unless you make two pairs. You will have a very weak kicker. If you pair your kicker you will more than likely get beat with an overpair. You can play unsuited Ace 9, 8, or 7 as long as there are no raises in front of you. Again, these hands usually spell trouble if an Ace flops. You need to flop two pair to be secure. If you don't, you may find yourself in the same trouble as the suited Ace hands.

Suited King
K-8s through K-2s

Suited cards with Kings play very similar to the Ace-suited hands. Your odds of making a flush are the same but you will not have the nuts if you do make it. (The nuts is the best hand possible.) In the case of a flush, anyone holding the Ace will beat you with the nut flush. Keep in mind, however, that one-third of the time you make a flush, the Ace will be on the board and you will have the nuts.

Connectors
8-7s, 7-6s, 6-5s, 5-4s and T-9, 9-8, 8-7

Little connectors can become powerful hands if the flop hits you. You are looking for a straight, or a straight draw, if the cards are unsuited, and the additional flush or flush draw with the suited connectors. Since many players will continue playing big overcards when the flop contains all small cards, it is possible to build a big pot. Since the value of these hands is dependent on the flop, it is important that you get in cheaply and release them quickly if the hand does not develop. These hands do not develop often, so you want to make sure that you have many players in the pot to make it worthwhile. Never play these hands against fewer than five players.

Gappers
Q-8s, J-8s, T-8s, 9-7s and K-9, Q-9, J-9

When your starting two cards have a gap between them, it will make it even more difficult to make a straight. When the hand contains cards with values Ten and below I will rarely play them with more than one gap unless I am in the small blind. The hands containing one big card with two gaps are playable but with caution as they are marginal at best. The suited gappers will give you the added potential for making a flush. Since you are playing these hands in multi-way pots with five or more players, the other hands can present trouble if you only pair one of the cards. If the flop contains big cards you will have a weak kicker with Kings, Queens, or Jacks. If you pair your 9 or 8 it will probably not hold up against a large field.

While playing in late position gives you the opportunity to play more hands, you still must be selective.

Here is a quick reference for late position.

Hand	Call—# Players	If Raised
6-6	Call—5 or more	Call 1 raise—6 or more
5-5	Call—5 or more	Call 1 raise—6 or more
4-4	Call—5 or more	Call 1 raise—6 or more
3-3	Call—5 or more	Call 1 raise—6 or more
2-2	Call—5 or more	Call 1 raise—6 or more
A-6s	Call—5 or more	Call 1 raise—6 or more
A-5s	Call—5 or more	Call 1 raise—6 or more
A-4s	Call—5 or more	Call 1 raise—6 or more
A-3s	Call—5 or more	Call 1 raise—6 or more
A-2s	Call—5 or more	Call 1 raise—6 or more
K-8s	Call—5 or more	Fold
K-7s	Call—5 or more	Fold
K-6s	Call—5 or more	Fold
K-5s	Call—5 or more	Fold
K-4s	Call—5 or more	Fold
K-3s	Call—5 or more	Fold
K-2s	Call—5 or more	Fold
Q-8s	Call—5 or more	Fold
J-8s	Call—5 or more	Fold
T-8s	Call—5 or more	Fold
9-7s	Call—5 or more	Fold
8-7s	Call—5 or more	Fold
7-6s	Call—5 or more	Fold
6-5s	Call—5 or more	Fold
5-4s	Call—5 or more	Fold
A-9	Call—5 or more	Fold
A-8	Call—5 or more	Fold
A-7	Call—5 or more	Fold
K-9	Call—5 or more	Fold
Q-9	Call—5 or more	Fold
J-9	Call—5 or more	Fold
T-9	Call—5 or more	Fold
9-8	Call—5 or more	Fold
8-7	Call—5 or more	Fold

"s" denotes that the cards are suited.

Chapter 15

Blinds

The blinds have the advantage of being in late position before the flop but the disadvantage of being in early position after the flop. Many players feel that because they put money in for the blinds that they must defend the blinds no matter what starting cards they hold. They will routinely call all raises, even with hands that they would not play from any other position. You must realize that once you put the money for the blinds into the pot, it is no longer your money. It belongs to whoever eventually wins the pot. Many players lose a lot of money from misplaying hands when they are in the blinds. In a ten-handed game, the blinds will account for 2/10 of your total hands. Playing every hand without regard to the action in front of you is no better than playing with the "any two cards can win attitude," which is essentially what you are doing

There are instances where you will want to defend your big blind against aggressive players who you know are just trying to steal your blinds. If other players discover that you do not always defend your blinds, they may just start making a positional raise every time you are in the blinds. This can be frustrating, but in many cases you can get the player to back down. To do this you must wait for a playable hand. Then, when the aggressor tries for a steal by raising the pot, you will re-raise him. In most cases a player will only try for a steal from late position when no one else has entered the pot. This means that you will most likely be heads up with this player. Since you will be the first to act after the flop you must come out betting. Unless the flop hits the other player he will usually fold and then think twice about attempting a steal in the future.

Big Blind

In an unraised pot playing the big blind is easy. You have a free ride. You have already made a bet so you only need to consider whether you want to raise or merely check your blind bet. In most cases you will probably want to just check. The reason for not raising with a strong hand is for deception. When a player raises from the big blind he is announcing to everyone that he has a powerful hand. You may find that you will not get too much action after the flop. If there are only one or two players, then you might consider raising to get more money in the pot, but you might be better off just calling and then trying a check raise after the flop.

If the pot has been raised, you need to determine where the raise came from and who made it. If the raise was made from a tight player in early position, you can pretty much determine that you are up against a strong hand. If a reraise occurs before it is your turn to act, you should not call unless you have a powerful hand of your own. If, however, the raise has been made from late position when no one else has entered the pot, you may be up against a player trying to steal and should treat it as such.

In a raised pot from the big blind with two or more players, you can call a raise with any pair, connectors, suited Ace or other middle position hands. Don't call a raise with a hand like J-2 or Q-5 or other hopeless hands. You want to defend your blind only if you have a chance of winning the pot not because you have already put one bet in.

Small Blind

One consideration when playing from the small blind is the limit of the game and the size of the small blind. In most Texas Hold'em games the small blind is half the size of the minimum bet but there are some low limit games where they are less than half. In a $2/$4 game the small blind is $1. In a $4/$8 game the small blind is $2. In these games, to call from the small blind you will only be putting in a half of a bet. In this situation, with an unraised pot you can play a little looser. You can play all of the late position hands. You can also play hands that include any two suited cards, smaller suited unsuited connectors or one gapped hands. In the small blind in an unraised pot you can also play any Ace or King. This does not mean that you would play a completely hopeless hand. A starting hand of deuce-7 off suit is still the worst hand in Hold'em whether you are in the small blind or not.

In the $3/$6 game the small blind is only $1 in most cardrooms. This means that you would have to put in two-thirds of a bet if you want to call. If this is the game you are playing, you should treat the small blind as if you were playing from late position. Just remember that you will have to act first after the flop. In a multiway pot you can also play small gapped hands.

Here is a quick reference for the small blind.

Hand	Call—# Players	If Raised
T-7s	Call—5 or more	Fold
9-6s	Call—5 or more	Fold
8-6s	Call—5 or more	Fold
7-5s	Call—5 or more	Fold
J-8	Call—5 or more	Fold
T-8	Call—5 or more	Fold

When I first started playing $3/$6 Texas Hold'em, I would routinely play almost all of the hands from the small blind. I soon discovered that this was eroding my session bankroll. In most cases, I would not hit the flop and I would have to check then fold. Many times I made only small pairs which would not hold up. Consider this, if the small blind is $1 and you fold your poor hands, you have saved $2. That money saved will cover your next two small blinds. In poker many times the money you save is as good as money you have won.

When the pot has been raised before you, don't think that you should immediately call just because you have a partial bet in the pot. In the $3/$6 game it will cost $5 to call a raise. Why would you want to invest $5 on a hand that you would not call a $3 bet with just because you already put $1 into the pot? With a raised pot, you should play the small blind as you would if you were playing from middle or late position.

Chopping

There will be times when all the players fold and the players in the blinds are the only ones left to act. In this situation there is an option called "chopping" which is allowed in most cardrooms. Chopping entails the big and small blinds folding their hands and taking back their blind bets. The hand is over, the button is moved and the next hand begins. Chopping is a personal decision that you must make. I have heard arguments on both sides as to whether or not a player should or should not chop. Some players always chop, while other players never chop.

The argument for chopping in a low-limit game is that there is not enough money with just the blinds to make it worthwhile to play out the hand. In a $3/$6 game there is only $4 in the pot. There is only $3 in a $2/$4 game. Some players feel that this is not worth the time or the risk to play the hand out.

There are some players, however, who never chop. Players who regularly play tournaments don't like to chop in live games because they feel that this heads up play will give them experience when they make it to the final table in a tournament. This is a valid point on their part.

Whether you decide to chop or not, you should stick with your choice for the entire session. I was playing in a game and one player chopped the pot on two occasions and then the third time he announced that he didn't want to chop this time and wanted to play it out. The big blind reminded him that he chopped on the two previous occasions and the player said he did not care and didn't want to chop this time. The big blind did not say another word about it but, instead of the folding as the small blind had hoped for, he raised. The small blind reraised and the big blind called.

The flop was all small, unsuited cards, and the small blind bet and the big blind called. Another small card came on the turn, and this time, when the small blind bet, his opponent raised him. Looking at the board cards the small blind reraised and the big blind called again. The river card again was small and no help. There were no straight or flush possibilities and the small blind bet and was raised. This time he just called. The big blind turned over pocket Aces. The small blind reluctantly showed his pocket Kings. Instead of stealing the $3 from the big blind, it had cost him a few dollars because he demanded to play the hand out.

Most of the players at the table felt that the small blind should have chopped this time since he had done so on the other occasions. They felt it was bad etiquette on his part to demand that the hand be played out. All of the players, with the exception of the small blind, were quite pleased with the outcome of the hand. They thought he was a poor sport for refusing to chop in this situation.

Live Straddle

There is a situation that you will encounter from time to time where the player next to the big blind raises the pot before the cards are dealt. This is known as a *live straddle*. Players who put up a live straddle are there to gamble. Most of the time they have just won a few pots and feel invincible or are trying to intimidate the other players. Sometimes the player may be on tilt or intoxicated. No matter what the reason, it is a bad bet that smart players don't make. When you encounter this situation you should play tighter than you normally would because it will cost you more money to enter the pot. If you have pocket Aces or Kings, you can confidently raise and know that the Straddler will call your raise.

Chapter 16

Building a Strong Foundation

What you are about to read is what I consider the most important concept in this book. It is easy to understand but will be difficult for some to execute. It is the key to winning play and, if you follow this advice, you will build a strong foundation for making you a winning player. From this base you will add all the other principals you learn about the game of Hold'em and soon you will be playing better than many of your opponents. I'm sure you have a desire to win. That is the reason you're reading this book. Are you willing to devote 50 hours of live play to improving your game? That is the amount of time most players will need to practice in order to develop good habits essential to winning play.

Fifty hours may seem like a long time to some. If you play only a few hours once a week you will be playing this style for about six months. But in the course of your poker lifetime, investing 50 hours of time is a small price to pay for the future dividends you will collect. The following advice is not merely about hand selection. It will help you develop a strong personal commitment to playing a solid winning game.

The starting hands in the chart may seem a little too tight to players who are used to playing any two cards in loose games. In reality, they are too loose for new players or players who have been playing indiscriminately and have been not been getting the desired results from their present play.

When I started learning to play Texas Hold'em, I was advised to play tight while learning the basics of the game. This advice was corroborated by several of the resources that I checked and backed up by some sound reasoning. The most important traits a player needs to develop in order to win are patience and discipline. Limiting your hand selection will help you do this. You will be throwing away many more hands than you will be playing. Waiting for the right hands to play will teach you patience. If you can discipline yourself to do this, you will develop a strong basic foundation that will improve your game. Let's take a look at the suggested hand selection to achieve this goal.

The suggested hands to play are the 20 strong hands that can be played from early position along with a few additional hands added in late position. Although these are early position hands they are spread out into the middle and late positions.

Early Position
Raise with A-A, K-K, and A-Ks from any position.
Call with A-K, A-Qs, K-Qs, and Q-Q and fold everything else.

Middle Position
Call with J-J, T-T, 9-9, 8-8, A-Js, A-Ts, Q-Js, A-Q, K-Q.

Late Position
Call with A-Xs, K-Ts, Q-Ts, J-Ts, A-J, A-T (note x denotes any card).

Play any pair and suited connectors if there are more than five players. If you play small pairs you must fold if you don't flop a set. Fold if the pot is raised.

I played only these recommended hands for the first 50 hours of play when I was learning the game. Limiting my play to these hands allowed me to concentrate on other fundamentals of the game. I used the time when I was not active in a hand to observe other players and practice reading the board. I found this was an excellent opportunity to observe what hands my opponents were playing. By the end of my session I could tell you what type of hands each player was entering the pot with. Knowing the standards of your opponents will tell you a lot if they later raise or call a bet.

The hands I did play, I played with confidence that I was making the correct decision. I was able to make my plays swiftly and accurately, which not only added to my confidence, but also helped to establish a strong table image. Above everything else, I was winning. The more I won, the more confident I became that I was following the right path in my quest to become a successful player.

I have to be honest. In the beginning there were sessions when this style of play did get a little boring. During one three-hour session I played only four hands in addition to my big blinds. I won three of these, which gave me a small profit for the night. The next day I joked that I had spent so much time folding, I didn't know if I had spent the previous night in a cardroom or a laundromat. Times like these will test your ability to stick with your game plan. You will be watching other players entering pots with pure garbage hands and thinking it might be time to loosen up a little. Don't do it! You are on a quest for excellence.

If you find you are getting bored, you should take a break. Get up and stretch your legs, go to the bathroom, grab a soda or just take a walk around the room. When you sit back down, try to concentrate more on reading the board, the players and other aspects of the game. Many players have no concept of pot odds. While you are limiting your play, you can also count the number of players in each hand and practice calculating the money in the pot. If you find you are still losing your commitment to your game plan, you should leave and call it a day. This is about patience and discipline. When you start to lose your patience, you need to have the discipline to leave the game.

There is nothing wrong with playing a tight game. Some players will argue that when you play tight, you will be missing out on opportunities to get full value from you play. I don't necessarily agree with that. Many low-limit games have enough action that will allow you to win a substantial number of chips using solid, aggressive, tight play.

There may be instances when you are playing with knowledgeable players and your tight play will be detected. If this happens, they will not call you as often when you do play a hand, but don't worry too much about it. I have found that this is offset by the number of players in low-limit games that have no concept about the style of their opponents' play. Most hands will go to the showdown in low-limit Hold'em games. You want to make sure you have the best hand at the showdown. You improve your chance when you start by playing strong, solid hands.

Game Plan

I use this tight playing style as my primary game plan. When I sit down to play with unfamiliar players I will start off in this tight mode until I get a feel for the other players in the game. As the game progresses, I may expand my starting hands to others in the chart but I always play the hands from proper position.

In a loose game, by starting tight and then playing a few more hands, it can convey the impression that I am actually playing the same loose game as everyone else. In reality, I am still playing solid starting hands but most players will not catch on to this.

Having disciplined myself to the tight playing style, I can switch back to the tighter mode at a moment's notice if the game starts getting too wild. It's like a fighter who can switch from righty to southpaw to keep his opponent off balance.

You want to be calling the shots. You don't want to get caught up in the wild and crazy playing style of the other players. You want them to fall into your game plan, not you into theirs. With a disciplined style of play you can achieve this.

Chapter 17
Probability and Odds

Probability and odds are the same thing but expressed in different terms. Probability is the chance that an event will occur and is expressed in percentages. The range of an event occurring is between zero and one. To simplify things and allow us to express percentages by using a whole number rather than a decimal we multiply by 100. If the probability of something happening were 0.6 percent we would say there is a 60 percent chance of it happening (0.6 x100 = 60).

Odds are the ratio between the number of times an event will occur and the number of times it will not happen. It is expressed with two numbers separated by a colon. If there is a 60 percent chance of an event occurring there is a 40 percent chance of it not occurring. We would express the odds as 6:4 for this event. To reduce this further we divide 6/4 and find the odds are 1.5:1. In poker and other gambling games, we use odds to express our chances of winning or losing. No matter how you express it, whether you talk percentages or odds, it is all based on mathematics.

There is a sign in the mathematics section of the Boston Museum of Science that reads:

"The theory of probability is nothing more than good sense, confirmed by calculations"

Sometimes when playing poker we throw our good sense out the window in hopes of an outcome that is contrary to sound mathematical principles. When this happens we are playing what I call a "wish" hand. You know the odds against you are astronomical, but you are wishing for a miracle draw. Occasionally you will make your hand, but in the long run you will lose more money.

Any time you are playing a drawing hand, the odds are against you. This means that you will not make your hand more times than you will make it. Most of the time the odds against you will be too large and it will be unprofitable to attempt to draw to the hand.

There will be other times, however, when the odds against you are offset by the money in the pot that you can win. In these situations it is correct to draw to a hand because are receiving the proper "Pot Odds."

Understanding Pot Odds

The Pot Odds is the relationship between the money in the pot and the price of a bet you must make to call. If the pot contains $36 and the size of the bet you must call is $6, we divide the $36 by $6 and we get 6, which means that the pot odds are 6 to 1.

Many low-, mid-, and high-limit Texas Hold'em players have no concept of pot odds and how it can affect their profitability. They don't understand the reasoning for playing drawing hands against a large field of opponents. Some hands that are profitable against many players will be a loser or a break even hand with fewer players in the game

First, I want to clarify that when we talk about odds and percentages we are looking at the long run. This is assuming that all possible outcomes will occur according to their probability. Anything can and will happen in the short run. Many players and experts have debated for years as to what actually constitutes the long run. Let's just assume we are talking about millions of hands. In the age of computers, we can simulate millions of hands in a short amount of time. That is more hands than any player will see in a lifetime. But you don't need to play a million hands to grasp the principle of pot odds. Here is a little experiment that you can try that will give you an idea of how the number of players can affect your winning with a hand that has the exact same odds.

This experiment simulates how the number of players will affect a hand that has odds of 3:1 against you. First of all, get a deck of cards and take out the four Aces, twos, threes and fours. You will have 16 cards. Then get coins or chips to use for the experiment.

There will be the four players in the game. Put out a stack of chips for each player. Each player puts one chip in the pot. Shuffle the 16 cards and deal a card. You can be player number one. Each time an Ace is dealt you win. If a 2 is dealt then player number two will collect the money in the pot. Likewise if a 3 or 4 is dealt the respective player will win the pot. Put another chip in the pot for each player and deal again. Keep repeating this until all 16 cards have been dealt. Notice what the results were.

Each time you win a hand you win three chips (one from each of the other players).
Each time you lose a hand you lose one chip.
You played 16 hands.
You won four hands and lost 12.
You won 12 chips for the four hands you won and lost 12 chips for the 12 hands you did not win.
You broke even.
The odds of winning were 3 to 1 and the pot odds were 3 to 1.

Now you will repeat the process but player number four will not bet. Anytime four wins put the three chips from the pot (yours and the two other player's chips) aside.

At the end of the16 hands notice the results:
You won the same four hands. But this time you only won 8 chips.
You lost 12 hands and lost 12 chips.
You are down 4 chips.
Your odds of winning were still 3 to 1, but the pot odds were 2 to 1.

Now put out another stack of chips. This time number four will again play as in the first round and a fifth chip will be put in the pot to simulate an additional player who will not win.

At the end of 16 hands:
You won four hands but this time you won 16 chips.
You lost 12 hands and lost 12 chips.
You won 4 chips.
Your odds of winning were 3 to 1, but your pot odds were 4 to 1.

With this example you can see how a hand offering the same odds can be profitable when played against a larger field but be unprofitable when you are playing against a limited field.

How to Determine Pot Odds

Many players feel that trying to keep track of the money in the pot is a difficult thing to do. I thought so too at first, but I then came upon an easy way to do this. First of all, it is easier to keep track of the number of bets instead of the actual money in the pot. After each betting round the dealer announces how many players are active in the pot. If there have been no raises you know how many bets have been put in by the number of players active in the hand. During the first betting round before the flop it is uncommon for players to fold once they enter the pot. If there has been a raise, just double the number of players and you know the total bets before the flop.

After the flop count the bets put in by the players in front of you during each round. When it is your turn to act you will have an accurate determination of the pot odds up to that point. You do not know what the players acting after you will do.

On the last two betting rounds the limits double and you must adjust your count to reflect this. It is easy to do. Just divide the number of bets that were made in half. Using the $3/$6 game, if there were ten $3 bets in the pot before the turn, it would now be converted to five $6 bets.

Implied Odds

There is a concept called implied odds for money you are sure will go into the pot after you act. This means that after you compute the odds before you act, you can add your opponent's future bet if you are sure there will be no raises. A simple example of implied odds would be if you held a small pair before the flop. If there are five players who have entered the pot before it is your turn to act, you are getting 5-to-1 odds. The odds for making a set are 7.5:1, which means you are not getting proper odds for this hand at this time. If you are sure that the players acting after you will call, or that there will be a bet made after the flop, you can consider these bets in the pot odds. These are implied odds.

This means you would try to calculate what you would win if your opponent bets and you make your hand and win the pot. If you were heads-up on a flush draw with one card to come, you would have nine outs and the odds against you are 4:1, which means that there should be $24 in the pot to give you proper odds. If there were only $21 in the pot you would only be getting 3.5:1. If, however, you know that your opponent will call a $6 bet if you make your flush, you can then add this to the $21 already in the pot thereby giving you an implied pot of $27. You then would be getting 4.5:1 odds for your $6 bet.

When you make your decision using implied odds you must be certain that you will win the pot with the best hand. You don't want to be drawing to a hand that is already beaten. This is known as drawing dead and will be explained in detail later.

Odds Charts

Here are a few charts that will show you the odds for certain circumstances that you will encounter while playing Texas Hold'em.

Starting Hands

There are 1,326 two-card combinations that can be made from a deck of 52 cards. Here are the odds for some of the starting hands.

The probability of holding . . .	Percent	Odds Against
A pair before the flop	5.9	16 to 1
Suited cards	23.5	3.25 to 1
Offsuit cards—no pairs	70.6	0.4 to 1
Pocket Aces—or any specific pair	0.45	220 to 1
All Ace-King combinations	1.2	82 to 1
Ace-King suited	0.3	331 to 1
A-A, K-K, or A-K	2.1	46 to 1
Single Ace	14.9	5.7 to 1
Premium hands—		
A-A, K-K, Q-Q, A-K, A-Q, K-Q	5	19 to 1

The Flop

With two cards in your hand there are 19,600 three-card combinations that can appear on the flop. Without considering your two pocket cards, there are 22,100 three-card combinations that can be made from a deck of 52 cards. This chart is based on 52 cards.

The probability that the flop will contain . . .	Percent	Odds Against
Trips—Three of a kind	0.24	424 to 1
A Pair	17	5 to 1
No Pair	83	0.2 to 1
Three of the same suit.	5	18 to 1
Two of the same suit	55	0.8 to 1
Rainbow—Three different suits	40	1.5 to 1
Three in sequence	3.5	28 to 1
Two in sequence	40	1.5 to 1
No sequences	56.4	0.8 to 1

Pocket Pairs

As noted, the probability of being dealt a pocket pair is 16 to 1. Being dealt a specific pair is 220 to 1. Your odds of getting pocket deuces are the same as getting pocket rockets. But two hands couldn't be farther apart. Here are some odds for your pocket pairs if you chose to continue to play them.

Holding a pocket pair the probability of flopping . . .	Percent	Odds Against
At least a Set or Higher	11.8	7.5 to 1
A Set—one of your cards on the flop	10.8	8.3 to 1
Full House	0.74	136 to 1
Quads	0.25	407 to 1

After the flop the probability of . . .	Percent	Odds Against
Set improving to Full House— Two cards to come	33	2 to 1
Set improving to Full House— On the Turn	15	5.7 to 1
Set improving to Full House— On the River	22	3.6 to 1
Pair improving to a set— one card to come	4.4	22 to 1
Pair improving to at least a set— if played to the river	19	4.2 to 1

Unless you hold pocket Aces there is always a chance that a higher card can appear in the flop. The lower your pocket pair, the more likely an overcard will flop.

Probability that a higher card will flop when you hold	Percent	Odds Against
Kings	23	3.3 to 1
Queens	43	1.3 to 1
Jacks	59	0.7 to 1
10s	71	0.3 to 1
9s	81	0.2 to 1
8s	88	0.1 to 1
7s	93	0.07 to 1
6s	97	0.03 to 1
5s	99	0.01 to 1
4s	99.7	0.003 to 1
3s	99.1	0.0002 to 1

Two Cards of Different Ranks

The majority of your starting hands will consist of two off-suit cards of different ranks. These hands can improve in several ways.

Holding different ranks

the probability of flopping	Percent	Odds Against
One Pair	29	2.5 to 1
Two Pairs	2	49 to 1
Trips	1.4	73 to 1
Full House	0.1	1,087 to 1
Quads	0.01	9,799 to 1
At least a Pair	32	2.1 to 1
No Pairs	68	0.5 to 1

With two cards to come

the probability of	Percent	Odds Against
No pair improving to at least one pair	24	3.2 to 1
No Pair improving to two pairs or trips	1.4	71 to 1
Pair improving to two pairs or better	20	3.9 to 1
Two Pairs Improving to Full House	17	5 to 1
Trips improving to Full house	33	2 to 1

Suited Cards

Whenever there are suited cards on board there is a possibility of a flush. You will be dealt suited cards 23.5 percent of the time. Here are the odds for making a flush.

With two suited cards

the probability of	Percent	Odds Against
Flopping two for a four flush	11	8.1 to 1
Then making the flush with		
2 cards to come (9 outs)	35	1.9 to 1
Flopping three for a complete flush	0.84	118 to 1
Flopping one of your suit	41.6	14 to 1
Flopping one and making flush		
on the river	4.2	23 to 1
Flopping none of your suit	46.6	1.1 to 1
Making a flush of a different suit		
(5 suited cards on board)	0.2	548 to 1

Connectors

There are many combinations of cards that you use to make a straight. It is easiest when you start with maximum connectors. Max connectors are two cards adjacent to each other with three cards open on each end. There are seven sets of max connectors. They are 4-5, 5-6, 6-7, 7-8, 8-9, 9-T, and T-J. The chart below shows the odds for certain situations.

Maximum Connectors the probability of	**Percent**	**Odds Against**
Starting hand.		
All—suited and unsuited	8.5	11 to 1
Starting hand. Suited only	2.1	46 to 1
Flopping an open ended straight draw	9.8	9 to 1
Then making a straight with 2 cards to come (8 outs)	31.5	2.2 to 1
Flopping an inside straight draw	21.6	3.6 to 1
Then making a straight with 2 cards to come (4 outs)	16.5	5 to 1
Flopping a straight	1.3	76 to 1

In some cases I have rounded the numbers instead of using two decimal places. For those wishing to do the calculations, the math used is explained in detail in *Hold'em Odds* by Mike Petiv.

Chapter 18
Calling

The main reason that poker players lose money is that they call too much with marginal hands. In Texas Hold'em the big blind constitutes a bet. After looking at your first two cards, you can fold your hand, call the blind bet or raise it. The expression "limping in" is used when you enter the pot by just calling the blind bet. Whether or not you enter a hand will depend on two important considerations. These are your position and how many players have entered the pot in front of you.

If you limp in from an early position, you have to take into account that a player may raise the pot after you. If this happens, you have to call the raise, fold or re-raise. In low-limit games, most players will call the raise rather than fold once they enter the pot. In deciding whether to play a hand you should ask yourself if you are willing to call if the pot is raised. If it is a marginal hand you may want to dump it instead of calling. In later position you will have more information about your opponents and the possible strength of their hands.

Number of Players

In middle and late position, the number of players who have called before you will affect your decision whether or not to play your opening hand. Big pairs can stand up on their own but when you have a small pair, connectors, or an Ace with a small suited card you will need to improve on the flop. These are drawing hands. You won't make them often but if the flop hits you they can turn into powerful hands.

Suppose you are holding

If an Ace flops, you have an Ace with a small suited kicker, but if you flop three spades, you now have the nut flush. If you do make a flush draw, and proceed to make your flush, you will have the nuts. Similarly, a small pair will probably not win on its own without improvement. In most cases, you will need to flop a set in order to win.

With these types of hands, you want to enter the pot with a minimum bet when possible. More times than not, you won't improve your hand, but if you do make your hand when there are a lot of people in the pot, the amount of money you make will compensate you for the times that you don't make the hand. If you have a drawing hand, you want at least four people in the pot when you are in middle position and five if you are in late position.

In a loose passive game, when you know that the blinds will usually play their hands, you can count them in, even if you act before them. Professional player and author Tom McEvoy coined the Two-Limper Rule in his book *Tournament Poker*. He writes that once two players have voluntarily entered the pot for a minimum bet, the pot has already shaped up to be multiway.

A tell is a mannerism or physical movement that can give you an indication as to a player's intentions. There are a few subtle tells that can help you determine if the players acting after you are going to call or fold. Obviously when a player throws in his hand out of turn you know they are folding. Other times they make a move that is almost as obvious. They hold their cards in a manner that lets you know they are going to throw them into the muck. You will see them with their cards in one hand and their wrist cocked back waiting to pitch the cards. This is a sure sign they won't be playing. If a player is not paying attention to the game or joking with another player while waiting to make his decision, there is a good chance he is merely waiting to toss in his hands.

The other side of this is when you see a player reaching for his chips before it is his turn to act. You know he will either be calling or raising. Another tell that someone will be calling is when he suddenly *pays attention* to the game.

Most cardrooms offer free copies of *Card Player* magazine. There have been many occasions when I have been in a game and players were actually reading at the table. If a player looks at his cards and then goes back to reading you know he is going to fold. If he looks at the cards and sets the magazine aside, you know he is going to play. This is a pretty obvious tell and I can only assume that these players do not realize the importance of the information they are revealing with this action.

When I started playing, I had a tell that would signal other players to my intentions. I was protecting my cards prematurely. When you are playing in a cardroom it is important to protect your cards at all times. Most players do this by putting a chip or coin on top of their pocket cards. I use a chip to protect my cards as well. What I did to give away my intentions was to look at my cards and then immediately cover them with a chip if I planned to play the hand. I would not cover them if I planned on tossing them into the muck. Luckily a good friend of mine saw me doing this and pointed it out to me. These are the types of things you should be looking for to determine a player's intention.

Most low-limit players do not give any consideration to the number of players in a hand, this is a concept that is either overlooked or ignored. Remember your big cards and pairs will win more against fewer players. Your drawing hands will play best against a lot of players. You need to know how many players are in the hand before you call.

Calling a Raise

When the pot is raised before the flop, you need to determine how your hand compares to that of the raiser. If the pot is raised before it is your turn to act, you will have to call the original bet and the raise. This is known as cold calling. If the pot were re-raised before it is your turn to act, you would have to cold-call three bets in order to enter the pot.

Unless you have a very powerful hand, you should not cold call any raises. You need a stronger hand to call a raise than you do to initiate one. If you have to cold call three bets you better have an extremely strong hand, such as, a pair of Aces or Kings or Ace-King suited, because you can pretty much figure that the player who re-raised has a very strong hand. These are the only hands I will cold call a re-raise with.

I have seen many players cold call two raises with hands such as unsuited K-J, Q-T, A-T, or weaker. This can be very costly.

The problem with hands like these is that even if you make a pair after the flop, you may only have the second best hand. If you hold no pair you will pair one of your cards about 32 percent of the time. That means the odds are about 2 to 1 against you pairing one of your pocket cards. If someone has a hand strong enough to reraise, they more than likely have you beat even if you pair one of your cards.

Since you don't have any money invested in a pot that is raised before it is your turn to act, you can merely fold and wait for another hand. Why take the chance of playing a marginal hand against a raise? If you are thinking about calling the raise you must consider the following:

From what position was the raise made?
If a raise comes from early position, you have to assume the player has a strong hand and he is trying to narrow the field. Most players raising from this position don't fear being re-raised. If the raise came from middle position in an unraised pot, the player could have a semi-strong hand and be trying to narrow the field. If a player is raising from middle position in a pot that has been called by several others, it is another indication of a strong hand. If the raise came from

late position in an unraised pot, a player may be trying to steal the blinds.

Who raised?

It is very important that you know who made the raise. If the player doing the raising is a very tight player, who only plays strong hands, you should have a powerful hand to consider calling. If the player is a maniac who is just looking for action, then he might be raising with any hand.

How many players have called?

The number of players who call a raise before you will determine whether you call the raise. If there are only a few players, you don't want to call with a drawing hand. If there are many players in the pot, and it has been raised, then you may be getting the proper pot odds to call. Sometimes the pot will get so big that it becomes what is known as "a protected pot." This means that you can be sure someone will be calling all the way to the end.

What is your position?

Before you call a raise, you need to determine how many players will be acting after you. Will any of them re-raise the pot? If you fear a re-raise, then your hand is not strong enough to call a raise.

What do you have?

Try to determine how strong your hand is compared to the raiser. Do you think you are beat gong in? Here again, it helps to know your other players. If you have a drawing hand and there are many players in the pot, you should be drawing to the nut hand if you are calling a raise. You won't make your drawing hand very often, and when you do, you don't want it to be second best.

Be Selective

Just as you are selective about your starting hands, you need to be equally selective about which hands you will call a raise with. Many players feel that once they call a raise, they must call a re-raise or two even though they are not getting proper odds to do so.

Chapter 19
Raising

Any player can raise the pot with any hand. It takes a weaker hand to initiate a raise than it does to call one. This does not mean that you should just raise the pot on a whim. There are five reasons to raise the pot when you are playing Texas Hold'em:

1. To get more money in the pot.
2. To narrow the field by eliminating other players.
3. To bluff.
4. To get a free card.
5. To gain information.

The two main reasons to raise before the flop are when you think you have the best hand and want to get more money in the pot, or when you want to narrow the field.

Bigger Pots

If you have the best hand, you want to get as much money into the pot as possible. Before the flop this includes your big pairs like Aces and Kings. Don't hesitate to raise or re-raise these hands. A pair of Aces is the strongest hand you can hold before the flop and a pair of Kings is the second best hand. These big pairs will not always hold up, especially against a lot of players. For this reason you want to get as much money in the pot for the times when they do hold up to win.

In a low-limit game, you should be careful with pairs of Queens and Jacks. Because many players will play a single Ace, you may find yourself in trouble with these hands if an Ace appears on the flop. Unless you think you can narrow the field, you may be better off calling with these hands. Many times players will raise with any two big cards such as King-Jack offsuit, only to see all little cards in the flop. They eventually end up folding when another player bets out or raises when the flop fits their particular hand. They could have saved a bet by simply calling before the flop. Poker expert Mike Caro feels that there is entirely too much pre-flop raising in most games. He feels that about 60 percent of the raising could be eliminated thus saving many players money. When you raise without a strong hand, you may just be making the pot bigger for someone else to win.

Narrowing the Field

You raise the pot when you want to narrow the field. Big cards hold up better against fewer players. The more opponents you can drive out, the better your chances of a large pair holding up. With many players involved in the pot, the chances of getting drawn out with a straight or flush are greater. Your position will greatly influence how many players you can drive out with a raise. Before the flop, if you raise under the gun or from early position, you may drive out players who are holding marginal hands. If there are a lot of players who have already called, your chances of chasing any of them out with a raise in a low-limit game are slim. You will find that once a player has called a single bet, they will not fold until they have seen the flop.

Bluffing

If your are in late position or on the button (Dealer), there is a chance that you can steal the blinds by raising if no one else has entered the pot before you. If you notice that the players to your left have previously folded their hands to a raise when they were in the blinds, this may work. You may have to test them. You should wait until you have a semi-strong hand to do this, in case they will staunchly defend their blinds with any hand. Many players feel that if they have money in the pot, they should play the hand no matter if it was raised or not. Some players will try an outright bluff by raising from early position. If you are in an extremely tight game, this may work, but for the most part bluffing with a raise before the flop should be avoided in a low-limit game.

Getting a Free Card

At first glance, the concept of raising to gain a free card may seem a little confusing but it can be a good value. Your position is an important factor when making this play and it works best when you are in late position and there are few players acting after you. When a player raises it usually means that he is holding a strong hand. In many instances, other players will check to the raiser on the next betting round for fear of being raised if they bet. If you have raised from late position and it is checked to you, you can also check and have the opportunity of seeing the next card for free.

This play is used a lot of the times on the flop when the betting limits are lower. In a $3/$6 game, the betting limit on the flop is $3; if you raise, it will cost you $6. The next betting round the limit goes to $6. If everyone checks to you on the turn because you raised, you can also check and you will get to see the river card for the price of your raise on the flop, which is $6. If you merely bet on the flop and then someone bets in front of you on the turn, it will cost you $9 to see the river card. By raising on the flop, you have increased the likelihood that it will be checked to you and you will see the turn card for free.

If you raise before the flop from late position, there is a chance that you can see all the way to the river card for free. You raise before the flop and then it is checked to you after the flop. If you check, you will get to see the turn card for free. In a tight game the players may again check to you after the turn card, which means that you can see the river card for free as well. You try to get a free card when you have a drawing hand and want to try to make your hand as cheaply as possible. However, you need to remember that while you are receiving a free card, all of your opponents are getting one as well. There is an equal chance that they will make their hands with the free cards. If you have raised, and a player bets before it is your turn to act, that usually means he improved his hand with one of the free cards. You may have to abandon your hand.

Gaining Information

Sometimes a player will use a raise to gain information about the strength of the other player's hands. This is usually done when the play is heads up. If you raise and are re-raised you can be fairly certain that the other player has a very strong hand. You want to do this on the flop before the betting limits double.

Chapter 20
Slowplaying

In Texas Hold'em you are not trying to win the greatest number of pots. You are trying to play correctly and win the most money. Two ways you can increase the money you win is with slowplaying and check raising. Both of these tactics have sometimes been referred to as "sandbagging" but there is nothing underhanded about either method. It is an acceptable practice used by smart players. Slowplaying is when you play a strong hand weakly to keep as many players in the hand, thus contributing to the growth of the pot.

You should slowplay your hand when it is very strong and you know that by betting all the other players will fold. Instead of betting, you would check and you would just call instead of raising if someone bets before you. You do this to conceal the strength of your hand. When you have the nuts or a monster hand that is unlikely to be beaten, you can give your opponents an opportunity to draw into a hand that will be second best.

If you held

and the flop was

you have a full house. Unless someone has A-A in the pocket you have the best hand. Someone holding two diamonds has a flush draw. A player with K-Q, K-T, or Q-T has a straight draw. In this situation you don't mind checking and giving a free card. If it is bet, you should just call since a raise may drive out the other players. Better to let someone make a flush or straight that will be second best to your full house. You will also get action from anyone holding a single Jack who has just made trips.

Another example of a hand to slowplay is:

If you held

and the flop was

Although most of the time you won't want to slowplay trips, it would be correct to slow play this hand. It is extremely unlikely that a player would be playing 7-2 unless he is the big blind. A player with the fourth Queen will have made top pair and will give you action. A player with two overcards such as A-K may be hoping to pair up. In low-limit games many players will play with a single Ace hoping to catch one on the turn or river. If an Ace falls on the river, you may even be able to check raise then.

When you slowplay, you have to be fairly certain that allowing someone else a free card won't give them a hand that can beat you. Many players slowplay hands that are only marginally strong and find that they pay the consequences for doing so. Small trips are very vulnerable and you should not slowplay them. Most of the time this would also hold true when you flop top pair. It will depend on the texture of the flop. Again your ability to read the board will be an important factor in deciding whether to slowplay or bet.

You don't want to slowplay AA before the flop unless your are in the blinds and want to disguise the strength of your hand. Aces play best against a small field. You raise to narrow the field. If you are in early or middle position, and decide to slowplay your hand it could be a costly mistake. If you merely call with AA, you are allowing everyone into the hand for a single bet. The more players in the hand, the more chances that one of them will flop a hand that can beat you.

If the flop is

someone holding 8-7 who may have folded if you had raised, has instead flopped a straight. Or the player who will play any connectors like 6-5 in an unraised pot has made two pair. You don't want this to happen. I have learned this from experience. After being burned by trying to slowplay pocket rockets, I now raise immediately with this hand.

It is better to bet out a hand and win a small pot than it is to slowplay a hand and lose a big pot.

Chapter 21
Check-Raising

Check-raising is when you check your hand and then raise when another player bets. In home games, the idea of check-raising is considered sandbagging and is frowned upon or even not allowed. However, it is allowed in most casino poker rooms and is a powerful tool to help you extract more money from your fellow players.

Check raising is a good way to get more money in the pot when you think you have the best hand. When you have a hand that can't be beaten you would want to slowplay, but if your hand is susceptible to a stronger hand you may want to utilize the check-raise. When you check-raise you are also looking to eliminate some of the players thus narrowing the field. This will depend on the position of the player you are check-raising.

A good opportunity for a check-raise comes when the player to your immediate left has raised before the flop. If you flop a strong hand and think that you have the pre-flop raiser beaten, it will be to your advantage to check-raise. If you bet, the player to your left may raise you immediately. This would force all the other players to either cold call two bets or fold. If you are certain he will bet, then you can check. Most of the other players will assume that the pre-flop player would naturally bet after the flop and many will call one bet. When the action gets back to you, a check raise will force them to call one more bet rather than two. Most players, having already called, will call a single raise.

If you are in early position and know a player in late position will bet, you can attempt to narrow the field by using a check-raise. If the player in late position has raised before the flop there is a good chance that many of the players will check to the raiser. When you check-raise, you are getting more money in the pot from the original bettor but you are also forcing some players acting after you to cold-call two bets. You would do this when you had a good hand but one that could be beaten by a player on a draw.

Suppose you were in the big blind and there are five players in the pot when a player in late position raises. You have:

The flop was:

You have made middle and bottom two pair.

You have a strong hand, but not one that you want to play against a lot of players. You check and, unless a player holds a single King, it is likely the other players will all check to the original raiser. The original raiser may have raised from late position with a pocket pair, or two high cards, in which case he will bet. You raise and now force all the other players to call two bets. A player holding only two big cards, or one on a straight draw, will not be getting proper odds to call the double bet and you will narrow the field to a heads-up situation where you are now a favorite to win.

Another situation where you may want to use a check-raise is to tame an aggressive player to your left. If you have been playing a tight game, checking and folding on the flop, you may become the target of a player who has taken notice of this. The player will refuse to allow you a free card by betting every time you check. All you have to do is check the next time you have a strong hand and then raise the player when he bets. If you do this a couple times, he will think twice about betting the next time you check, not knowing if you have a legitimate hand or not.

I discovered how effective this was the first time I played Hold'em in Las Vegas. I sat in on a game and could tell several of the players knew each other. Obviously, I was one of the tourists and the player to my left bet every time I checked. I was in the game about an hour when I finally got a strong hand. This time, when the player bet I check-raised him. He called but then mucked his hand as soon as I bet on the turn. The next time I had a hand, I repeated the procedure and from that point on I got no more indiscriminate bets from this player.

In order for a check-raise to work, you have to be certain that a player who acts after you will bet. If you check a good hand with the intention of check raising and everyone after you checks as well, you have defeated the purpose. Worse still, you have given all the other players a free card, which could make them hands that beat you. If you have any doubts that a player acting after you will bet you would be better off to just come out and bet the hand. This will assure that anyone on a draw will either have to pay up or get out.

Some players will try to see the rounds cheaply, unless they have a big hand. I have had many situations in which I have attempted a check-raise only to have it fail when the other players simply checked along with me. I have adopted a motto that I use: "When in doubt, bet it out!"

Calling a Check-Raise

If you are on the receiving end of a check-raise, you have to ask yourself, does this player want me to call? Again, you have to look at the position of the check-raiser to determine if he is attempting to bluff you into folding, or trying to suck you into putting more money in the pot.

Take a look at the board and determine how your hand stands up against the best hand that can be made. If the check raise came on the turn when the limits were double you can figure that the raiser is trying to get you to call two bets on the turn and another one on the river. Unless you have a powerful hand of your own, this is usually a good time to get out while you can do so cheaply.

Chapter 22

Bluffing and Semi-Bluffing

In low-limit games, bluffing will usually be an exercise in futility. The reason for this is that there are usually many players calling to the end. It is easier to bluff one or maybe two players, but it will be almost impossible to bluff everyone in a multiway pot. If there are any calling stations in your game, you should not even attempt a single bluff. If you find yourself heads up with a tight player, you may succeed but should refrain from all out bluffs in most situations. There will usually be someone wanting to "keep you honest" by calling your bet. That said, there is a type of bluffing that you can incorporate into your game; it is called semi-bluffing.

Poker expert/author David Sklansky coined the phrase semi-bluffing. It is a profitable technique that is used by advanced players. Unlike a bluff, when you have nothing, semi-bluffing is done when your hand is not strong enough to win the pot at the time, but does have the potential of improving to the best hand. If you bet, you are hoping that the other players will fold and you will win the pot without going any further. If you are called, then you still have a chance that your hand will improve to be the best hand.

Many semi-bluffing situations will come when you have a flush or straight draw. Raising on the flop could win you the pot or get you a free card.

If you held

and the flop was

you should bet if you are the first one to enter the pot. If someone else bets, you can semi-bluff by raising with this hand. If no one has a King, the other players may figure you for a pair of Kings and fold. However, you have many ways of improving your hand. Any heart will give you a flush. There are three Aces that will make you two pairs and two 7s that can make you trips or quads.

Semi-bluffing with a straight draw when you don't have a pair is not as strong a play but is still correct in most situations.

If you held

and the flop was

you only have two overcards. If you were to raise from early position, you may either win the pot or get to see the turn and maybe the river card for free. You have eight outs to make a straight.

Raising with Ace-King before the flop is technically a semi-bluff. While it would be possible to win with Ace high, you will probably need to improve this hand. If, however, you raise and everyone folds, you win.

Occasionally you will come across a circumstance when the winning hand is on the board, although it is not the nuts. This could be when the board shows a straight or a flush. There are several players in the hand and it looks like it will be a split pot.

The board is:

If you are last to act and everyone has checked, you can bet and possibly cause another player to fold. You are bluffing that you have the Ace of hearts. If any players fold, you will be splitting the pot with fewer players.

Calling a Bluff

Just because you will not be doing much bluffing does not mean there won't be any going on in the game. Some players in low-limit games think that bluffing is an important part of the game and they will try it whenever possible. If there is a maniac in the game, this player may try to run over other players by raising and bluffing. If it succeeds, he will keep doing it. You can't call these players with anything just to try and catch them bluffing. Wait until you have a legitimate hand and then nail them with a raise of your own.

Be aware that many players will try to bluff on the river. If they have a busted draw, they may try betting or raising to win the pot. If you have a legitimate hand, and there is substantial money in the pot, you should call. If the pot contains $90 and it will cost you $6 to call a raise, you are getting 15:1 odds. It is better to lose $6 if you call and lose, than to forfeit $90 if you toss away the winning hand.

Chapter 23
The Flop

Choosing to play a starting hand is the biggest decision you will make while playing Texas Hold'em. Deciding whether to continue playing after seeing the flop will be your second biggest decision. It can also be one of the most costly decisions if you continue after the flop with an inferior hand. It is said that the flop defines your hand. That is because after the flop your hand will be 71 percent complete. Where does this figure come from? Assuming you play your hand out to the end, it will consist of seven cards. After the flop you have seen five cards or 5/7 of the final hand, which is equal to 71 percent. With this much of your hand complete you should have enough information to determine whether to continue.

Deciding to continue playing after the flop is not as easy as choosing a starting hand. There are only 169 two-card combinations for starting hands, but there are 19,600 three-card combinations that can appear on the flop. Combine this with the two cards in your hand and there are 2,598,960 five-card combinations that can be made. After waiting patiently for the correct starting hand, the sad reality is that most of the time you won't like the flop.

Poker writer Shane Smith coined the phrase, "Fit or Fold." You will want to use this criterion when deciding to continue playing the hand. If the flop fits your hand, you will continue playing it. If the flop does not fit your hand, you must fold. The flop can fit your hand three different ways.

It improves your existing hand.

The flop may make you a complete hand that is capable of winning the pot without any further improvement. You could make top pair, two pair, trips or any other complete hand.

It gives you a good draw.

The flop may give you a good hand to draw to. This could include a four-card flush or straight draw. With three or more players in the hand you will generally be getting correct odds to draw to this hand.

It beats the board.

The cards in your hand will beat the cards on the board. If you hold an overpair to the board, you have the top pair in the pocket. Sometimes with just overcards higher than the board cards, you can continue playing.

This may sound very simplistic since there are other considerations you need to make even if the flop fits your hand. The make-up of the flop will be a determining factor as to whether you continue playing. Many players in low-limit games will play any two suited cards. If the flop shows two cards of the same suit, there is a good chance one of the other players could be on a flush draw. If the flop gave you an open-ended straight, you could be drawing dead if the other player makes a flush.

Players in low-limit games also like to play any Ace, regardless of the kicker with it. For this reason you have to be very careful when you see an Ace flop. If you are holding a small or medium pair, and there is a bet and raise with an Ace on board, you should fold. If you entered the pot with a small pair in late position, you should fold if you do not make a set on the flop.

Many times the flop will not fit any player. All the players will check the flop looking for the turn or river cards to improve their hands. It's for this reason that you want to play solid starting hands. If you have a card in your hand that is higher than any card on the flop, it is called an overcard. When everyone misses the flop and checks, you may pair an overcard on the turn or river to give you the winning hand. You should be aware that the more people in the hand, the more of a chance there is that someone will make a pair. If someone bets, and you hold only overcards then your safest move will be to fold.

Learning to read the board is an important skill you need to develop even if you follow the fit or fold method for playing your hand. You need to determine where your hand stands in relation to the best hand on the board. This is not to imply that someone will have the nuts for every hand, but you need to determine the strength of your hand compared to all of possible hands. The best hand after the flop is a huge favorite to be the winner at the end.

I wanted to find out how often the best hand after the flop went on to win the pot, so I ran a series of computer simulations using the Wilson Turbo Texas Hold'em software. The first simulation I ran was of five million hands with ten players using the low-limit profile. The best hand after the flop won 70 percent of the time. I repeated the simulation against a field of ten average players and found that the best hand after the flop won the pot 74 percent of the time. I ran a third simulation and found that heads up against one opponent it won 75 percent. These figures are a strong incentive to fold if the flop doesn't fit your hand. Playing wish hands, hoping for a miracle draw, will cost you a lot of money during your playing career. *If you have nothing after the flop, fold your hand and save your money!*

There is no single correct way to play your hand after the flop. There are just too many variables to take into account. You should also be aware of some other considerations.

How many players are in the hand?
If you are on a draw, you want enough players in the hand to make it worth your while to continue. If you have top pair, you want to limit the field if possible, because the more players in the hand the bigger the chance that someone will complete a drawing hand.

Your position.
You should always be aware of your position. The number of players acting after you may have a bearing on whether you check, bet or raise. Any time you are in late position you have an advantage. The later your position, the stronger your advantage.

Was there a raise?

If there was a raise during the previous round you need to know who made it and what position the raiser is in. Is this player a solid player or habitual bluffer?

How much money is in the pot?

You need to know approximately how much money is in the pot at all times to determine if you are getting the correct odds to continue playing. Usually three or more players will give you the odds you need after the flop.

General Guidelines

I have advocated seeing the flop as cheaply as possible. If you decide to continue playing once you see it, then it is time for you to become the aggressor and take the lead. If you are first to act, before you check, ask yourself if you would call a bet if someone else bets after you. If you would, then you should bet. You can't determine the strength of anyone else's hand by checking. If they bet, you still have no idea what cards they may be holding. Instead, you should bet, and if you are raised you have information that your opponent probably has a strong hand. You can fold, call, or raise accordingly. Since the betting limits are still low, the flop is the time to use a bet to determine the strength of your opponent's hands. If you are in later position, you may want to raise to narrow the field or to get a free card on the turn.

You don't want to play your hand the same way every time. If you are too mechanical, a sharp opponent will be able to read you. These are some general guidelines you can use in determining how to play your hand after the flop. Before we go any further, keep one thing in mind.

A winning player is the one who knows when to let go of an unprofitable hand.

Chapter 24

Overcards

An overcard is any card in your hand that is higher than any of the cards on the board. I start with overcards because you will end up with them a good percentage of the time if you are starting with two big cards. If you have two different cards in your starting hand you will pair at least one of them 32 percent of the time. This means that 68 percent of the time you will not flop a pair and you will be left holding two overcards. Many players will call or even bet with just overcards. Some will call with just one overcard such as the any Ace scenario I already covered. This is not correct and will cost you money in the long run.

Playing overcards is one of the costliest hands in low-limit games. Players will raise before the flop with two big cards and then continue betting and calling it all the way to the river against a couple of players hoping to make a pair. With overcards, you stand to lose a lot of money if you don't make your hand. If you do win, it will probably be a small pot as there will not be much action. If there are several players in the hand betting and calling, you can pretty much surmise that one of the players has caught a piece of the flop.

If you held a hand such as K-Q or K-J off suit, and the flop brought medium or small cards take a close look at the board. If there are two or three connecting or suited cards you could be up against a straight or flush draw. There is also a chance that a player has flopped a set. After the flop, if you do pair on the turn, which will only happen about 24 percent of the time, you may be drawing dead.

A-K is frequently misplayed because a player will raise and re-raise with this hand before the flop. When they do not pair on the flop many players will not want to let this hand go. They will play it as if it were a pair of Aces or Kings—betting and calling against several players. Most of the time it is best to check with this hand. If you raised before the flop and are in early position against only one or two players who you know are tight then you may want to try a semi-bluff to see if they will fold. If you are raised you must get out immediately. If you are in late position and it was checked to you, the best move may be to check as well. This will eliminate the possibility of getting caught by a player who is trying for a check raise. If you do not pair on the turn, it will be time to fold if there is a bet.

This isn't to say that you should never play overcards. Obviously you'll continue playing any two overcards if it is checked to you. However, betting with them is not your best option. If you have two suited overcards and there is one of your suits in the flop it may be correct to call a single bet to see the turn. You might pair one of your cards or, if another of your suit appears on the turn, you may you may be able to make a backdoor flush. This will be rare and there is still the possibility that you will be drawing dead to another player.

Single Overcard

While I'm discussing overcards I need to state again that it is not correct to play a single overcard such as any Ace or King unless you have a flush or straight draw to go with it. I have seen players holding a single Queen or Jack with an off suit medium or small card call all the way to the river. With no draw possible, the best they can hope for would be trips or two pairs or a single pair with a weak kicker. With two cards to come, the odds of making trips or two pairs is 71:1. That will only occur about 1.4 percent of the time.

Pairing your overcard, with two cards to come, will only happen about 12 percent of the time and if you do make a pair you will have a weak kicker. A single overcard is a garbage hand that belongs in the muck pile with the rest of the trash. Save your bets and save your money.

Chapter 25

Pairs

When you start with two different cards the odds of flopping a pair are 2.5:1, which means it will happen about 29 percent of the time. If you do flop a pair you hope to match the highest card on the board which will give you top pair. If you saw the flop with a solid starting hand there is a good chance you will have the top kicker as well. When you flop the top pair with the top kicker you have a very strong hand and will probably have the best hand at the moment.

Top Pair Top Kicker

The best hand to have is A-K when either an Ace or a King flops. This will give you top pair and kicker. If the King flops you can't be beaten by a player holding a single Ace. If an Ace appears on the board he will have a pair of Aces, but you will have top two pairs. This isn't the case if you hold less than A-K.

   If you held

and the flop was

you would still have top pair and kicker but would have to be concerned if a King shows up on the board. The same can be said if you held A-J and a Jack flops. You would have to be concerned about a King or a Queen appearing on the board. You also need to be aware of any possible straight or flush draws that could come along on the flop. Any time there are two of a suit or connecting cards, there may be players on a draw. That is why you want to act aggressively with top pair by raising so you will make it very expensive for them to draw out on you.

Since you can be beaten, you don't want to slow-play this type of hand. If you try to check-raise and no one bets you will be letting your opponents have a free card that can beat you. In early position I will always bet with top pair. If I am in middle position with top pair and top kicker I will usually raise if there has been a bet in front of me. If the board looks harmless, and there are only one or two players in the hand, I will just call a bet from last position if I think a player will bet on the turn and I can raise then.

One situation where you would probably not want to raise is if you made a weak top pair playing from the big blind. If you held Q-9 and the flop was 9 high you should bet the top pair but be prepared to fold if you are raised. A player may have limped in with a pair of Jacks or Tens and now has top pair in the pocket. If you are called and an overcard falls on the turn be prepared to check and fold if there is a bet.

Top Pair Small Kicker

If you flop top pair and have have a small kicker, then you have a weak hand. This will happen when you enter in late position with hands like Axs or Kxs. (Note: The xs represents any small card that is the same suit as your Ace or King.) This hand is known as a trouble hand because with an Ace or King on board there is a good chance that one of your other opponents has made a pair as well. When you make top pair and have no kicker your best course of action is to check if you are in early position. If everyone else checks, then you can figure no one else is holding a pair and you can bet on the turn. If you are last to act you can also bet top pair with no kicker. Anyone slow-playing this hand is making a mistake. If there is betting or raising in front of you, then you should save your money and fold.

Middle and Bottom Pairs

If you pair any card other than the top one you will have either a middle or bottom pair. The most common situation occurs when you are playing smaller connectors from middle or late position. Many players hate to fold anytime they have a pair, but in most situations it is the correct play. With a large number of players in the hand, there is a good chance that someone has made top pair.

If you held

and the flop was

or

the pairs of 9s would be unplayable.

There will be some situations where it is correct to continue with middle or bottom pair. The first requirement is that the pot is extremely large to be giving you correct odds to call. If you have middle pair with an overcard kicker you have five outs to make either two pair or three of a kind. The odds are about 4:1 against you, which is the reason the pot must be big enough to justify this. If you have middle or bottom pair with a suited overcard and one card of your suit appears in the flop you will also have a chance to make a backdoor flush.

Overpair

An overpair is a pair in the pocket that is higher than any cards on the board. It is better than top pair because anyone with top pair will give you action without knowing they are beaten on the flop. The larger your pair, the more confident you can feel. Obviously the best hands are pocket Aces or Kings but even these are vulnerable in a large field. If your overpair is Queens or Jacks, you will also have to worry if an Ace or King comes on the turn or the river. You should play an overpair as aggressively as you would top pair, if it is bet in front of your raise. If it is raised in front of you, go ahead and re-raise; you want to narrow the field as much as possible.

Underpair

An underpair is a pocket pair lower than the highest board card. It can be very costly if you are the type that will not give them up. When an overcard flops and there is betting you are probably beat. With small pocket pairs, if there is any type of action you should just fold. Your odds of making a set on the turn are 22:1. The pot would have to be huge justify this call. If you are last to act and it is checked to you with only one or two other players in the hand, you may try to bet if these are tight players. You may win the hand right there. If there are more players or you are in the hand with a calling station, just take the free card and save your money. The exception to this is when your underpair is one of the paint cards, Jacks, Queens, or Kings. If you are first to act, go ahead and bet.

If you held

and the flop was

go ahead and bet; but if your are raised, then you will have to back down. If your bet narrows the field and you are heads up with another player he could be holding a Ten. If there is more than one caller, you should be prepared to dump your smaller underpair. With more players in the hand, there is a greater chance that you are up against the top pair.

Two Pairs

There are three different ways to make two pairs. If your two pocket cards are different and you match two cards on the flop then you have a concealed two pairs which is a strong hand. You can also have a pocket pair and have another pair appear on the flop. This is not as strong a combination as the concealed two pairs. The third possibility is when one of your pocket cards pairs the board when there is also a pair on the board.

Concealed Two Pairs

When the two cards in your hand pair up with two board cards you can make three different two pair combinations. You can have the top two pairs, bottom two pairs, or top and bottom pairs.

Top Two, Top, and Bottom Pairs

When you hold the top two pairs and there are not three suited or connecting cards, you most likely have the best hand at the time.

If you held

and the flop was

the only way someone could have a set is if he held pocket Queens, Jacks, or 7s. Any player pairing the Queen or Jack will surely give you action. You want to get as much money into the pot as you can. If you are in early position and you think someone will raise then go ahead and attempt a check-raise. If not, bet. If it is bet or raised before you, go ahead and raise or re-raise. In this example, if the 7 matched the suit of the Queen or Jack you are looking at the possibility of someone on a flush draw. You want to make it very expensive for them to try and draw you out.

When you have the top and bottom two pairs you also have a strong hand. Your strength will come from your top pair. The bottom pair could be compromised if a higher pair shows up on the board. In the above example, if you got a free ride from the big blind and your pocket cards were Q-7 you would have top and bottom two pairs. If another Jack or a pair higher than 7 is made with the turn and river cards, then your pair of 7s is compromised and is worthless.

Bottom Two Pairs

When you match the middle and bottom cards on the flop you have the bottom two pairs. It can be beaten if any player has the top pair and matches one of your middle or bottom pairs. This will happen more often when the flop brings higher cards.

If you held

and the flop was

Many players will play K-T or K-9, and your two pairs could be beaten. In this case you could also be beaten by anyone who has any Q-J combination.

You should never slow-play when you have two pairs. There are just too many instances when things can go wrong. If the board pairs, and the pair is higher than either of your two pairs, the strength of you hand has been compromised. Many times when you make two pairs, you will have started with connectors or gapped cards. If you make two pair you should also be aware that the board cards might give another player a straight draw. If two suited cards appear on the flop you need to be thinking about a possible flush. For these reasons, when you have two pairs you want to play as aggressively as you can to narrow the field and to get as much money into the pot for the times that your two pairs do hold up.

When the Board Pairs

Some players will make two pairs that include a pair on the board. They either have a pair in the pocket or they pair one of their pocket cards. They fail to realize that everyone else also has at least a pair. In this situation, you essentially have a single pair. If it is higher than the board pair you still have a playable hand. If your pocket pair is lower than the board pair you will save money by folding this hand whenever you are in this situation. Poker expert Mike Caro astutely points out that if the board pairs it is bad news unless it helps you exclusively. There are also other considerations you need to be aware of when a pair is on board:

How many people are in the hand?

Again we look at the importance of knowing how many active players are in the hand. The more players who see the flop, the more likelihood that one of them have made trips. If there are five or more players, it is almost certain that someone will benefit from the pair. If it is not you then you must be prepared to fold if there is betting and raising.

What is the strength of the pair?

The higher the value of the pair also relates to the chance that someone will have made trips. If it is an Ace or a face card, there is more of a chance that one or two players will be holding one of these cards. It is possible for two players to make trips when there is a pair on board.

Is a Full House possible?

Whenever there is a pair on board there is always the possibility that a player has a full house or can make a full house. You should pay close attention to the relationship of the other cards on board to the pair. If there is a connecting card or an Ace then there is a greater chance of a player holding a potential full house.

If the flop was

many players will play connectors as a starting hand. In this case a player with 7-8 in the pocket will have made a full house. If the flop was 8-8-3, there is less likelihood of a player having 8-3 in the pocket.

There should also be a full house alert that sounds whenever you see an Ace and a pair on the flop. Since many players will play an Ace with any card, there is the possibility that they have made a full house if they match their second card.

Here is a money-saving tip I learned the hard way: If you have a four flush and there is a pair on board, fold your hand if the pot is multiway and there is a lot of action. Any time there is a pair on the flop the value of a flush draw is greatly reduced. You could be drawing dead against a player with trips drawing to a full house. You will make the flush about 35 percent of the time. However, your opponent will turn his trips into a full house about 33 percent of the time. The odds are about the same, but you have the lesser hand. The money you save by folding this hand will outweigh the money you will lose in the long run in this situation. Whenever you see a pair flop on board you should proceed with caution. Be prepared to fold if you are not helped by it.

Chapter 26

Trips vs Sets

Not all three of a kind are the equal. If you have a pair in the pocket and a third card appears on the flop, you have a set. If you have a card in the pocket that is matched by a pair that flops, you have trips. Many players feel that both are three of a kind and should be treated the same. This is not true. A set is more powerful than trips. Two people can have the same trips. When there is a pair on board another player could have the fourth (case) card giving him trips as well. Only one player can have a set.

A Set

The strength of a set lies in the fact that it is well disguised. Any innocent looking flop could actually make a set for anyone with a pocket pair. In fact, most of the time when we have a pocket pair, we will need to make a set to have a winning hand. As much as we love pocket Aces and Kings, most of the time our pocket pairs end up in the muck pile. The sad reality is that unless we make a set, our pocket pair will usually not be strong enough to win on its own merits. Unfortunately you can only expect your pocket pair to turn into a set about 11 percent of the time. The good news is that anytime you make a set on the flop you will win about 80 percent of the time.

Because the set is so difficult to read most players will not put you on this hand. Go ahead and bet. You will get action from any one with top pair. If there was a raise before the flop and you are sure there will be a bet you could try for a check raise. I prefer to bet this hand hoping that the player with top pair will raise me. I will then smooth-call the raise and save the check-raise for the Turn when the betting limits have doubled.

You should not slow-play a set especially if the flop is showing two suited cards or a possible straight draw. A set is strong but can be beaten, so you don't want to give any free cards in this situation. You are better off getting money into the pot. An exception is when you are absolutely sure the flop has not given anyone a drawing hand. If I have pocket Aces and the flop is something like A-8-3 rainbow, I will check from early position to give the impression that I am afraid of the Ace. If I am in early position, I will check to give the impression that I am afraid of the Ace. If it is checked around I will bet on the turn. If it is bet before me I will just call on the flop and then raise on the turn.

Trips

Trips are not as strong as a set because every other player is sharing that same pair on the board. If another player has the same pocket card and makes trips it could come down to the kicker deciding the hand. The higher the cards on the board the more chance that another player will make trips as well. This is especially true if a pair of Aces or Kings come on the flop. Since many players will play a single Ace, a flop that contains a pair of Aces is bound to produce two players with trips

When you make trips on the flop you will improve to a full house about 33 percent of the time. However, it is possible that another player will make a full house as well. Anyone with a pocket pair has a chance for a full house when there is a pair on board even if you hold trips. It will then come down to who has the higher full house. You would lose if you held

and the flop was

and another player holds

    Whenever there is a flop containing high cards and a pair there is also the chance that your trips could be beaten by a straight. Suppose you were getting a free play from the big blind.

    If you held

and the flop was

it is likely that another player could be holding a hand such as A-T, A-Q, Q-T, or T-9, which would give them a straight draw. Anyone holding two spades would also have a flush draw.

This is the reason you want to play trips as fast and hard as you can most of the time. Bet, if you are first to act. If there is a bet in front of you, raise, and if there is a raise go ahead and re-raise. You want to get money in the pot and narrow the field as much as possible. Many times a player with a pocket pair will bet or raise. If you can get this player heads up you are a 2-to-1 favorite to win.

Chapter 27
Flush Draws

If you do flop a four flush you will make a flush about 35 percent of the time. Which means the odds are 2-to-1 against you. In low-limit games with many players seeing the flop, you will be getting correct odds to continue with the draw. Still, you have to be fairly certain that your hand will win if you do make your flush.

Since many players will be playing any suited cards, you want to make sure you will have the highest flush should the third suited card come on board. You also want to be playing hands that will offer you other opportunities to win if you do not make the flush. By playing proper starting hands you should have this covered. Big cards can win the pot if you pair them without making a flush, and suited connectors can make a straight.

If you hold

and the flop is

you have top pair with top kicker along with a four flush. You have nine cards that can make you a flush along with three Aces and two Queens that can improve your existing hand.

Saving Bets

If you do make a flush and raise the pot be careful if you are reraised. Suppose you hold

and the board is

and there is a bet in front of you. Possibly someone made it with a pair of Queens or a small flush. You raise with your Queen-high flush and get re-raised. Do you think the player would be re-raising you with a Ten-high flush? Although it is possible that a player in a low-limit game would do this, its time to back down. You should check on the river as you are probably beat and do not want to bet and get raised again.

When there is a pair on board you have to be aware of a full house. The higher the pair, the more likely that someone has made a full house.

If you were the big blind and entered the hand with

and the board shows

you made your flush on the turn. However, if there is a bet and a raise in front of you, you can be pretty sure that your hand is a loser. Anyone holding a King and a Jack would have made a full house. Any two hearts with one card being an 8 or higher will have you beaten. As much as you hate to lay down a small flush in this situation, it would be correct to do so. With one card to come, it will be very costly to cold call a raise and then call on the river only to find out what you already suspect.

Another bad situation that calls for backing down occurs when a fourth suited card shows up on board. You make your flush on the turn and the river brings another suited card. There is now a four flush on the board. Unless you have the Ace, it is advisable to just check this hand. Many times with three suited cards on board you will see a player calling bets with just the Ace of that suit. It doesn't happen often but you will save money by checking when it does.

If you did bet, and the player does not have a flush, he would more than likely fold anyway so you have more to lose than gain by betting.

Semi-Bluffing

If I'm in late position and I have a four flush, and I am holding the Ace, which will give me the nut flush if I win, then I will raise on the flop. There are two reasons to do this. If I do make my flush on the turn I have gotten more money in the pot. If I don't make my flush I have a chance of seeing the river card for free. Many players will check to the raiser. If this happens I can simply check if I have not made my flush. I then see the river card for the price of a single bet on the flop.

Chapter 28
Straight Draws

Straight draws are some of the most deceptive hands to read. An innocent looking flop can spell potential disaster if you are not paying close attention to the board. In low-limit games players love to play any connectors and sometimes gapped cards. If you see three cards in sequence and there is action, it is easy to determine that someone has made a straight. But you also need to give the board a closer look to determine if there is any inside straight draws possible. There are several different types of straight draws you can have.

Straights can be a profitable hand but they can also be easily compromised and beaten by bigger hands. Before you continue drawing to a straight you must be fairly sure that it will win if you make it. If the flop brings two suited cards, or a pair, you may be drawing dead to a flush or full house. If you do make your straight, you want to play it fast and aggressively. If you are certain of a bet, you can check-raise, but don't slow pay this hand. Don't give anyone a free card in case the board pairs or a flush card falls giving someone the potential cards to beat you.

With all drawing hands you want to make sure that you are getting proper pot odds for your draw. This means that you want to have many people involved in the hand. This is usually the case in most low-limit games. Four or more players seeing the flop and continuing on should afford you the proper money in the pot to continue with a straight draw.

Open-Ended Straight

The open ended-straight draw is the most common straight draw you will be attempting.

   If you held

and the flop was

you can make your straight with either a King or an 8. Since there are four of each you have eight outs to make your hand. You have a 31.1 percent of making your hand, which means the odds are only 2.2 to 1 against you. If you do make it, there is no way you can lose to a higher straight.

Inside Straight

In games like draw poker you never want to draw to an inside straight. It is not a profitable hand. In Hold'em, where the pots can be very large, it is sometimes correct to make this draw providing that you are drawing to the nuts. You don't want to waste money on an inside draw if you can be beaten if you make it.

If you hold

and the flop is

 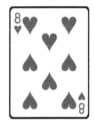 

with an inside straight draw you are 11-to-1 underdog to make the hand. You should probably try to get in cheaply. If there are five or more players before the flop and you are in early position, you should check. If enough players bet after you, the odds will justify putting in your bet. If you are in late position, and it is checked to you, you can check and see the turn for free.

Low-End Draw

It is all right to draw to an inside straight in Texas Hold'em but you don't want to draw to the low end. In the example above, if the cards were reversed and you held the 9-8 and the Q-J were on the board, then you would not attempt the straight draw looking for a Ten. If you did make the straight someone holding an Ace-K or King-9 would have you beat. If there are three straight cards on the board you should also pass if you have the low end and there is a raise or two. With the community cards involved, when three straight cards are on the board, it is likely that someone will have the cards at the higher end.

If you are in late position and hold

and the flop is

and there is a bet, you should fold this hand. This hand is essentially the same as an inside draw. If a 6 does come on board, it is likely that the original bettor or one of the other Players is holding J-Q. If a Jack comes on the board, a single Queen will beat you. This is a very costly draw and you should learn to avoid it.

Flopping a Straight

If you hold connectors at the low end of the sequence and make a straight on the flop, you may be in for a big loss if someone holds the connectors for the higher end. This hand should be played cautiously. You should be prepared to let it go if you have another player raising you. I learned this the hard way early in my playing career.

The second time I played in the casino I was trying my best to keep my concentration on the game and avoid making any mistakes. I was playing in a $3/$6 game at the Mohegan Sun in Connecticut. I had been playing a fairly tight game but I was determined to play the hands I entered aggressively. I was ahead a few dollars and it was my turn as the big blind. I looked at my pocket cards and saw:

 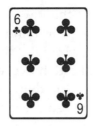

If I had not been the big blind I would have folded without a second thought. There were five callers but no raises so I checked the option and waited for the flop.

The flop was

I had to look twice. YES! I had flopped a straight. On the outside I was very cool as I bet my hand. Two players folded and the other three called my bet.

The turn was a 2 and no help.

I bet again and this time everyone folded to the guy on the button. To my surprise he said, "raise" as he put his $12 in the pot. I thought to myself, *What's this joker trying to do? No way is he going to bluff me out of this pot.* "Reraise!" I called as I slid my $12 in the pot. He called and the dealer turned the final card. The 3 of hearts and no help again.

This was going to be a nice pot. I was only thinking about how lucky I was to have flopped the straight. I once again confidently bet my hand. The other player looked at me and slid $12 in the pot and said, "Raise."

Ok, I thought. *I'll just call his raise and collect my money. Won't this guy be surprised when I turn my cards?* My smugness and euphoria was short lived as I looked in utter surprise as he turned over the Ten and Jack of clubs. He had also flopped a straight and he had the high end.

I had heard the low end of a straight called the "Idiot End." Now I knew why. I was blinded by my own straight and I neglected to look at the possibility of another player holding a J-T. I was the idiot in this case. I did, however, learn an important, albeit expensive lesson. You can be sure that I will not make that mistake again. From that day on I promised myself that I would always pay closer attention to the board especially when I am raised while holding the wrong end of a straight.

Chapter 29
The Turn

The turn is appropriately named. It is the turning point of the betting rounds when the price of a bet doubles. This is the time to separate the pretenders from the contenders. It is the time to get out if you hold only a marginal hand. After the turn you have a hand that is 86 percent complete.

Since the betting limits double on the turn, the pot odds are now cut in half. In a $3/$6 game if there were $30 in the pot you would be getting 10:1 odds on a $3 bet. Now that the bets are $6 you are only getting 5:1. You might not be getting the correct odds to stay in with a drawing hand. For example, after seeing the turn, if you are trying to draw to an inside straight you only have four outs. The odds are 10.5 against you. If you are only getting 5:1 in pot odds and you should give it up.

In the simulations I ran to determine how often the best hand would win after the flop, I also checked how often the best hand would win after the turn. Using the low-limit profiles, in a field of ten players, the best hand after the turn held up 79 percent of the time. Against a field of average players, the best hand on the turn went on to win 82 percent of the time.

With the addition of the turn card, there are more possible hands that can be made by the cards on the board. Keep in mind that if you are playing correctly, you will only see the turn if you have a good hand or a strong draw. Most of the time you will have folded after the flop. If you have come this far, you should be aware that many times the turn card will not improve your hand. It is now up to you to decide to continue or not. The betting limits have just doubled. It's not too late to get out fairly cheaply if you don't have a good chance of winning or are not getting correct odds to continue. Here are a few general guidelines for playing your hand on the turn.

Checking

If you have an open-ended straight or flush draw, you want to see the river as cheaply as possible. In this instance it is usually best to check. If someone bets, and it is raised, you can get out without putting any money in the pot. If there is no raise and there are three or more players, you can call the bet because you should be getting correct odds to do so.

Betting

If you plan on calling a bet then, in most cases, you should initiate one rather than checking and calling. Your bet may cause other players to fold. By betting you are also making them wonder about the strength of your hand. If you check and then call you are telling your opponents that your hand is not very strong or you are on a draw.

When you have top pair, trips, or another hand that you think is best at the time but could be beaten, then you should bet. You don't want to give anyone a free card to possibly draw you out on the river. Make them pay to continue with the hand if they are on a draw.

When you have the nuts or a very strong hand, you want to get as much money in the pot as possible. You may be tempted to try for a check-raise. Unless you are certain that an opponent will bet, you are better off betting your hand outright. When you bet your hand on the turn, you will get other players with drawing hands to call you because they are hoping to make their hand on the river. If you check and everyone else checks, you have missed an opportunity to get their money in the pot. If you bet and they fold, so be it. If you check and then bet the river, these same players will fold anyway if they did not make their hand, and you have lost a bet they would have put in on the turn.

Semi-Bluffing

One situation that occurs fairly often in tight games is that everyone will check the flop. If they do not make a hand they will then check again on the turn. This presents a good opportunity for you to semi-bluff. In many instances players are just looking for a reason to fold and you may win the hand right then and there. If I am holding a four flush with an Ace or King in late position, I will bet this hand. Another opportunity to semi-bluff presents itself when you hold the Ace and there are two matching suited cards on the flop, giving you a three flush. If a third suit appears on the turn you can raise. No one will know that you do not have a flush and you may win the pot right there. If not, you still have 19.6 percent chance of making the nut flush on the river.

Calling

Most of the time you will call a bet in front of you if you were planning to bet it anyway. This doesn't mean, however, that you will automatically call a raise. First you must consider who made the raise and what position that player is in. If a player raises on the turn from early position it usually means he has a strong hand. You should not call a raise with just one pair on the turn if there are many players in the hand. If the raise was made from late position, it could be a semi-bluff, but calling a raise with only a pair can be costly. If you have a drawing hand you should be certain you are drawing to the nuts, or close to it, if you are calling a raise.

Here is a money saving tip. Don't call a bet on the turn with just two overcards. In the long run you will lose more than you will win, even if you pair one of your cards on the river. If there are several players in the hand, you are probably drawing dead trying to make a high pair. *Drawing dead* means you are drawing to a hand that you can't win even if you make it.

Raising

If you have two pairs or better and think you have the best hand, then you should raise. This will get more money in the pot and hopefully narrow the field for you. If you only have top pair and a player bets into you, that usually means he is not afraid of top pair. You should not raise in this situation. It is better to just call and see what the river card brings.

Scare Cards

Any time the board pairs, or there is a third suited card on the turn, you need to re-evaluate your hand. If you held the best hand after the flop, it is possible that it got demoted with the turn card. If you made a straight on the flop but the turn brings a third suited card, you could be up against a flush. If you bet this hand and are raised you can be pretty sure that is the case. If the board pairs and there is action you might be looking at a full house. If there is a bet and raise before it is your turn to act, you will be able to get out of this hand cheaply. You may hate having to fold a straight, but it will be a lot more expensive to call the river with a hand that was beaten on the turn.

Make Your Choice

Most of the time when you call a bet or raise on the turn, you are committing yourself to betting on the river as well. With only one card to come it should be apparent how your hand stacks up against the board. Since the betting limits are double, a mistake on the turn will cost you more than one on the flop. Don't play wish hands or hands that you are drawing dead to. A winning player knows how to release a marginal hand and the turn is definitely the time to do it.

Chapter 30

The River

If you have been playing properly, you will not see the river card unless you have a strong hand that is a favorite to win or you have a draw to a winning hand. Once the river card is turned over you know exactly what you have. If you were drawing to a hand, you know whether you were successful or not. By reading the board, you can determine the strength of your hand and know how it compares to the nuts.

Betting the Nuts

If you have the nut hand, your only concern is how to get the most money in the pot. This will depend on the number of opponents still active in the hand as well as your position. If you are first to act in a multiway pot and there is another player who has been the aggressor, you may be able to try for a check raise if you are certain that they will bet. If you are uncertain that another player will bet or are heads up against a single player then you should always bet.

If you are not first to act and there is a bet in front of you and more players to act after you, then it will usually be correct to just call. If you were to raise in this situation you may force out the other players in the hand who have yet to act. By just calling there is a better chance of them calling as well. If you are last to act, and everyone has checked to you, then obviously you would bet and hope the pot is big enough to justify your opponents making a call.

Betting First

Anytime you bet a strong hand you are betting for value to get more money in the pot. In most situations when you are first to act on the river, you should bet any hand that has a possibility of winning. Some times a bet will drive out other players who might be holding a hand that is better than yours. The other reason to initiate the betting with a marginal hand is to force out any player who may have been on a draw and missed. If you check, you are opening the door for a player who would have folded to bluff on the end.

Raising

Sometimes it may be to your advantage to raise even if your hand is not the nuts. Some players will bet on the river when they are playing overcards or have missed their draw. If you suspect that a player may be bluffing and you act right after them, a raise may drive out any players after you and narrow the field putting you heads up against the original bettor. For this to work, you have to know the other players and be certain that your hand can win heads up against the original bettor. In most cases you will only raise on the river when you are certain that you have the winning hand.

Two Mistakes

When you get to the river there are two mistakes that you can make. One is to call a bet, which will cost you the price of a bet. The other is to fold your hand, which will cost you all the money in the pot. Obviously, folding your hand will be a far more costly mistake than merely calling a bet. It is said that a good Hold'em player earns about one big bet an hour. If you call and lose, you could be giving up an hour's profit. If you fold a winning hand, you are giving up many hours worth of profit. This is not to say that you should never fold when you are beaten. However, if there is a chance that you could win, then most of the time you will be justified in calling on the river. The reason to make the call comes down again to pot odds.

Pot Odds

In low-limit games the pots can get very large. You have a lot of players seeing the flop and many staying to see the turn. By the time the river card is dealt, you will probably be getting the correct odds to call with any hand that has a possibility of winning. Look at this example. You are in a $3/$6 game and you get to the river and there is $60 in the pot and you are last to act. There are two other players still active in the hand. Before any betting takes place you are getting 10-to-1 odds. If the first player bets there is now $66 in the pot. The second player calls and brings the pot up to $72. It will cost you $6 to call as well. You are now getting 12-to-1 odds for your call. If you made this same call 13 times and lost 12 times but won once you would be even. You would lose $6 in 12 attempts or $72 when you lost, but would win $72 when you won. If you were to win this bet once in 12 tries, you would be ahead of the game by $6.

When in doubt it is better to call than fold on the river.

Scare Cards

You should always look closely at the river card and try to determine how it could help someone's hand. If everyone checks on the turn, and there is a bet from early position when a third suited card falls, you can be pretty sure you are up against a flush. If the board pairs on the turn, it could give someone a full house. Because of the any Ace mentality in low-limit games, you should also be cautious when an Ace comes up on the river. A player with a small pair and Ace kicker could have made two pairs. Many times a player who has lead all the way with top pair will lose to a pair of Aces on the river. Another situation that involves an Ace appears when a fourth suited card falls on the river. If a player has a small flush, many times he loses out when the fourth suit makes the nut flush for a player with the suited Ace.

The more players you are up against, the more likelihood that the river card has helped someone. If you are first to act against only one player, you can bet out and give the impression that the scare card has helped you. Sometimes this may be enough to convince the player to fold if the card was no help to them.

Checking

There will be situations when you may be better off checking. If you miss your draw but have overcards that could win if others missed as well, a check is in order. If a scare card comes, and you know that a player will only call your bet if they know they can beat you, then you should check. This will save you a bet.

Watch the Action

If you are a tight aggressive player you will not be seeing the river too often. Most of the time you will be watching from the sidelines—"watching" being the key word here. You should be paying attention to the game even when you are not involved in hand. It is extremely important to be watching the play on the river. This is when the players will be showing their starting hands. This will help you determine the caliber of player you are up against, since you will be able to determine who is playing solid hands and who is playing with the "any-two" mentality.

In low-limit games you will be drawn out on the river more than in higher limit games. This is a reality and a fact of life. Don't get upset when this happens. In the long run you will win more with solid play than the player who constantly bucks the odds.

Chapter 31

"That's the Nuts!"

My late grandfather Bill Ferguson was one of the greatest card players I've ever known. He wasn't a high-stakes player but he loved cards and played just about every card game imaginable. He was skilled at every game he played and was as proficient at Poker as he was at Cribbage or Bridge. Besides his love of cards, he loved people and he had an uncanny ability to read people as well as he could read the cards on the table.

Combining these two talents made him a formidable opponent to anyone challenging him to a game of cards. In a cribbage match, he would have his opponent's hand counted for them before half the cards were played. In poker, he could spot a bluff or calculate the pot odds with a quick glance. His "poker face" consisted of a smile on his face and a gleam in his eye. This threw off more opponents trying to read him, as they could never tell what lay beneath that happy exterior. His love of cards spawned some of the metaphors that he used in daily life. One expression in particular that he used to say amused me as a young child. Pop would often see something he liked and say; "Now that's the nuts!" I would laugh but I was confused why he thought something nice was nutty. One day I asked him why he called things he liked nutty.

He looked at me and said, "When you play poker and have a hand that can't be beaten it's called the nuts. So when I say something is the nuts it means it's the best there is." A few years later when he taught me to play poker I finally understood the relevance of that term.

When you are playing Texas Hold'em you should be able to look at the cards on the board and determine "the nuts."

Look at this example.

If the cards on the board were

and you held the

the best hand possible is a heart flush. Since you hold the Ace of hearts you have made the highest flush possible. You have a "Nut Flush." In an ideal situation your opponent will have a lesser flush and give you plenty of action. When you have the nuts you want to get as much money in the pot as you can. If you have players in the pot that you know will bet, you can go for a check raise. If you are in a very passive game and the players are likely to check along, then it would be better to bet it out and hope that one of the other players raises you. Then you can re-raise.

There will be situations when you have the very best hand after the flop. Some players mistakenly identify this hand as the nuts and will bet it without giving any regards to the cards that come on the turn and the river. This can be a costly mistake when it happens.

I was playing in a game and limped in from late position with:

There were several players who called the pot but there were no pre-flop raises. The flop was:

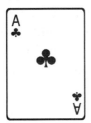  

Two players checked then the next player bet, and I called with my bottom two pairs. The player to my left raised the pot and the two players who checked, folded. The original bettor and I called the raise. The game had been fairly loose and the player could have been raising with a pair of Aces. By reading the cards on the board I knew it was possible that he could also be holding an Ace high straight.

The turn card was

This gave me a full house of Queens full of Tens. The player to my left bet and I raised. The player who had previously raised, re-raised me and the original player folded. The best possible hand on board was now Aces full of Queens. The other player could not have four Queens as I held one of them. I did not think he had pocket Aces because this player had previously raised before the flop with any pair from any position. I re-raised and he re-raised me back. I called because I knew that my hand was strong but it was not the nuts. The river card was a 3 that did not help at all. I bet and he merely called me.

I turned over my Queen-Ten and he turned over his King and Jack. He looked at my full house and was shocked. He said, "I flopped the nut straight! I thought you had a straight as well and we were going to split this pot."

Another player quipped, "You may have had the nuts on the flop but you forgot about the turn and the river cards!"

By thinking that he had the nuts, he re-raised in situations where he should have just called. He admitted later that he misplayed the hand. There will be situations when you will flop the absolute nuts that won't change, but other times you have to be aware that the turn and river card may change the best hand on the board.

Chapter 32
Board Reading

Along with being able to determine the best hand, you also need the ability to identify all the combinations of hands that can be made from the board cards. It is extremely important that you can determine how your hand stacks up against the other possible hands that your opponents may hold. This is known as reading the board. In Texas Hold'em, your ability to read the board is one of the most important skills you can develop.

Players in low-limit games will often play starting hands consisting of any two cards. It will be harder for you to try and read their hands because of this. It is therefore important that you be aware of all the possibilities and determine how strong your own hand is relative to the cards on the board. This is actually not hard to do. With a little practice you can master this part of the game. You can practice every time you play whether you are active in the hand or not. This will not only give you practice in reading the board but also make you aware of the types of hands your opponents are playing.

Without considering your pocket cards, take a look at five cards that represent the flop, turn, and river. (Note: In all explanations below x represents any other card.)

If the board cards are

the possibilities for this hand in order are:

Three of a Kind

Aces if you had A-A
Jacks if you had J-J
7s if you had 7-7
5s if you had 5-5
Deuces if you had 2-2

Two Pairs

Aces and Jacks if you had A-J
Aces and 7s if you had A-7
Aces and 5s if you had A-5
Aces and Deuces if you had A-2
Jacks and 7s if you had J-7
Jacks and 5s if you had J-5
Jacks and 2s if you had J-2
7s and 5s if you had 7-5
7s and Deuces if you had 7-2

Pairs

Aces if you had A-x
Jacks if you had J-x
7s if you had 7-x
5s if you had 5-x
Deuces if you had 2-x

That is a pretty innocent and straightforward set of board cards with limited possibilities for a big hand. There are situations where the board cards will throw up a red flag and make you look for potential bigger hands.

When the Board Pairs

Whenever there is a pair on board, there is a potential for a big hand. When you see a pair on board there is the potential for either four of a kind, or more likely, a full house.

If the board cards are

the possibilities include:

Four of a Kind

Four Queens if you held Q-Q

Full House

Aces full of Queens if you held A-A
Queens full of Aces if you held A-Q
Queens full of 8s if you held Q-8
Queens full of 4s if you held Q-4
8s full of Queens if you held 8-8
4s full of Queens if you held 4-4

Three of a Kind

Queens if you held Q-x, except for Q-4, Q-8, or A-Q

Two Pairs

Aces and Queens if you held A-x
Queens and 8s if you held 8-x
Queens and 4s if you held 4-x

Four of a kind is a rare hand. If you held a Queen, you know there is no chance of anyone having a four of a kind. When you see a pair on board, your first thought should be a possible full house or three of a kind. If you did hold a Queen and raised with your trip Queens, you should be very concerned if you are re-raised. Would your opponent be re-raising if he couldn't beat trip Queens? Probably not.

Suited Cards on Board

Whenever there are two or three cards of the same suit on board you should immediately consider the possibility of a flush. I have been in many low-limit games where the players will enter the hand with any two suited cards. Any time there is a raise after a third card of a suit falls, then you can almost be sure someone has a flush. Usually if a player checks after the third suit hits the board, they do not have the flush unless the three suited cards are on the flop and they are slow playing the hand. When the third suited card comes on the river and there is action, you can pretty much count on someone having the flush. Sometimes players will be so excited when they make a flush that they will neglect to further read the board and are surprised when they get beat out by a higher hand. This can happen if the board pairs after there are three suited cards on board.

If a player held

and the flop was

the player has just flopped the nut flush.
    If the turn and river cards were

he would lose to a full house if another player had:

Kings full of Tens if he held K-T
Kings full of 9s if he held K-9
9s full of Kings if he held 9-9
3s full of Kings if he held 3-3

When the Board Has Two Pairs

Any time the board has two pairs, you have double the chance of a four of a kind or, more likely, a full house. All a player needs to do is to match one card of either pair to make a full house. If there is considerable action when the second pair hits the board, you should be ready to fold. Even if you make a full house you need to realize that unless you made the nut full house, you can be beaten. I learned this the hard way when I was new to the game.
    I was playing in a game at a casino in Tunica, Mississippi. I was in the big blind and held:

The flop was

and the turn was

I was ecstatic and I decided I would try for a check raise. I checked, two players checked as well, and the third player bet. Two other players folded and I raised when it got back to me. The two other players folded and the original bettor called me. It was now heads up.

The river card was

I bet and my opponent raised me. What was he doing? I had a full house so I re-raised him. He re-raised me and I called.

I turned over my

He then turned over

It was an expensive lesson that I still remember to this day. I did not pay close attention to the cards on board. I should have realized that it is a lot easier for more than one person to have a full house when there are two pair on the board.

Straight Cards on Board

Straight draws are very deceptive and sometimes difficult to read. Whenever there are three sequenced cards or two cards with a gap of three or less, there is a potential for a straight. In fact, all flops that don't contain a pair can make a straight with the fourth card except for: K-8-3, K-8-2, K-7-2, and Q-7-2

Many players will play starting hands that have connectors suited or unsuited, or two cards with a single gap. If you see three cards in sequence and there is action you should be thinking straight. If you hold connectors at the low end of the sequence and make a straight, you may be in for a big loss if someone holds the connectors for the higher end.

Double inside straights are a little more difficult to read. If you misread the board you can be surprised by a hand you never expected.

If the board cards are

a player holding any J-9 combination would have the nut straight. Remember the board cards will not be in any specific order and you will have to look closely to see all the possibilities.

The most dangerous board is one that consists of high cards that are paired and suited. Many players will play any two high cards especially if they are suited. Look at the possibilities for this board.

If the board cards are

here are the possibilities:

Straight Flush

Royal Flush if you held A-J of spades
Straight Flush if you held J-9 of spades

Four of a Kind

Four Kings if you held K-K

Full House

Kings full of Queens if you held K-Q
Kings full of Tens if you held K-T
Kings full of 9s if you held K-9

Flush

If you held any two spades

Straight

Ace high if you held A-J
King high if you held J-9

Three of a Kind

Kings if you held K-x
Queens if you held Q-Q
Tens if you held T-T
9s if you held 9-9

Two Pairs

Aces and Kings if you held A-A
Kings up if you held any pair or a single Q, T, or 9

With these possibilities you can see why a board of all big cards can make for a very large pot and a potential big win or big loss if you are on the loser.

Learning to read the board is just a matter of practice. Knowing some of the red flags makes it easier to quickly evaluate how your hand will stack up against your opponents' hands.

Chapter 33
Drawing Dead

"Drawing Dead" is the term used when your hand will be a loser even if you draw the cards to complete or improve it. Your ability to read the board will help you determine if your are drawing dead or not. You also need to be aware of the actions of the other players still in the hand. While you can't be 100 percent certain that someone has made his hand, you can surmise that someone has made a hand if he is betting and raising.

When you determine that you are drawing dead then it is time to muck your hand and move on. Many players in low-limit games will refuse to accept the fact that they are beaten and will continue to play only to discover that their hand is second best.

Pocket pairs are one of the hands that a player will continue to play even when he could be drawing dead. An example of this is when there is a straight or flush draw on the board but a player will continue in hopes of making a set, even though he will be a loser if he makes it. I have seen this numerous times especially with big pocket pairs when players will refuse to lay down their hand. A player has

The board shows

A player bets and another player raises. There is a possible flush and a possible straight on board. The betting indicates that the raiser probably has one or the other. The player with the two red Aces is drawing dead. If the Ace of spades falls it will put a fourth spade on the board. If the Ace of clubs falls he will still lose to a flush if another player has two spades, or to a straight if a player is holding Q-T in his hand. Let's look at another situation using the same board cards.

A player holds

If the player is drawing to an inside straight hoping for a Ten he would really only have three outs. He would not want the Ten of spades to fall, as this would also put a four flush on the board. Again with this hand a straight would be beaten by a flush. If there has been action you should save money and muck this hand.

Drawing to the low end of a straight is another hand when you are more than likely drawing dead. That is why you are advised against doing it. You should also consider that you might be dead when a pair shows on the board and there is considerable action. By paying attention to the board and the other players, you should be able to make a better determination as to whether you are drawing dead or not. You won't always be right but it is usually better to be cautious and fold rather than calling and coming out second best.

Chapter 34

Know Your Outs

If you were trapped in a burning building and there was only one way out, your odds of survival would not be very good. If there were two ways out, your odds would greatly improve. Your odds of survival would improve with each additional way out of the building.

In poker your outs are the unseen cards that will complete or improve your hand to make it the winning hand. Each additional card or "out" will improve your percentage of surviving the hand and coming out a winner. I'm not trying to compare playing a poker hand with a being trapped in a burning building. (Although some people might feel that way.) I just want you to view outs as your indicator of success or failure when determining whether or not to continue with a hand.

Your skills at reading your opponents and reading the board are important when figuring your outs. You need to assess your opponents' hands and try to determine what they may have. Your perception of their hands will form the basis for deciding what you need to beat them. You then need to read the board and determine which cards will give you the winning hand. The cards that you determine can improve your hand to a winner will be your outs. You can figure your odds of improving your hand once you determine your number of outs. Unfortunately, knowing your number of outs and the percentages for making a hand will not be much help if you do not read your opponent's hand correctly. Your opponent may have a hand that you can't beat even if you complete your hand. This is known as drawing to a dead hand and was covered in the previous chapter.

Reading your opponent's hand is a skill that you need to develop. You will become more proficient with experience. It is not an exact science and you will be wrong many times. This should not stop you from trying. Each time you play a hand you must consider the strength of your hand in relation to the cards on the board and what hand your opponent could be holding. You then figure the percentage for improving your hand based on the number of outs you have.

Some hands, such as a four-card flush are fairly common and you will easily remember your outs for that hand. Other hands are less common and will take a little thought on your part. Let's take a look at a few examples to help show you how to determine your outs.

Example One

If you hold two suited cards and the flop brings two other cards of the same suit, you have a four-card flush. There are 13 cards in each suit. You have four of them, meaning that there are nine left in the deck. This means that you have nine "outs" to make your flush. With two cards to come, you have a 34.97 percent chance of making a flush. The odds are 1.86 against you making it. After the turn, with only one card to come the odds are 4-to-1 against you.

Example Two

You have an unsuited Queen and Ten and the flop is A-9-8 rainbow (all different suits); you have an inside straight draw. The turn card is a "blank" which means it is no help to your hand. If you perceive that your opponent has a pair of Aces, you will need to make a straight to beat your opponent. There are four unseen Jacks that will give you a straight. You have four outs to make your hand. With one card to come you have an 8.7 percent chance of making it and the odds are 10.5-to-1 against you.

Example Three

You have the King and Jack of hearts. The flop is Queen of clubs, Ten of hearts and 2 of hearts. You have nothing at this point but you have an open-ended straight draw. You can get one of the four Aces or one of the four 9s left in the deck for a total of eight outs. You also have a four-card flush giving you an additional seven outs for a total of 15 outs. There are nine hearts left in the deck but you have already counted the Ace and nine of hearts for your straight draw. With 15 outs you have a 54.1 percent chance of making a straight or a flush. The odds against you are only 0.81-to-1, which means you have a pretty good chance of drawing a winning hand.

The math used to determine the percentages and odds of making a hand is not difficult if you have a strong math background, but I found the calculations a little difficult to do without the benefit of a calculator. Let's take a look at the flush draw. You have four cards to the flush after the flop. You know there are 13 cards of each suit. You have four of them, which means there are nine remaining in the deck. You have two cards in your hand and there are three cards that were flopped so there are 47 cards remaining in the deck.

First we determine the odds for not making this hand. You have two chances to make the flush with the turn card or river card. For the turn you subtract the nine flush cards from 47 and you get 38/47. For the river you subtract nine from the 46 remaining cards to give you 37/46. Multiply 38/47 * 37 /46 = 1406/2162 = .65 or 65 percent of not making a flush. Subtract 65 from 100 and you see there is a 35 percent chance of making a flush.

I know that I am not capable of figuring odds like when I'm sitting at the table. So one of the alternatives would be to memorize a chart for all the outs. The Out Chart shows you percentages and odds for each number of outs after the flop with two cards to come and after the turn with one card to come.

Out Chart

Number of Outs	After Flop Two Cards to Come		After Turn One Card to Come	
	Percentage	Odds to 1 Against	Percentage	Odds to 1 Against
1	4.3	22.4	2.2	44.5
2	8.4	10.9	4.3	22.3
3	12.5	7	6.5	14.4
4	16.5	4.1	8.7	10.5
5	20.3	3.9	10.9	8.2
6	24.1	3.1	13	6.7
7	27.8	2.6	15.2	5.6
8	31.5	2.2	17.4	4.7
9	35	1.9	19.6	4.1
10	38.4	1.6	21.7	3.6
11	41.7	1.4	24	3.2
12	45	1.2	26.1	2.8
13	48.1	1.1	28.3	2.5
14	51.2	0.95	30.4	2.3
15	54.1	0.85	32.6	2.1
16	57	0.75	34.3	1.9
17	59.8	0.67	37	1.7
18	62.4	0.6	39.1	1.6
19	65	0.54	41.3	1.4
20	67.5	0.48	43.5	1.3

You will find that you can easily remember a few of the most common situations for outs such as the four flush or straight draw, but there has to be an easier way than memorizing the figures for every number of outs. The good news is that there is a way to get a good estimation of the odds.

The Rule of Four-Two

The rule of four-two, as I like to call it, is an easier way to figure the odds for any situation where you know your outs. It is not completely accurate but it will give you a quick "ballpark" figure of your chances for making a hand. Here is how it works.

With two cards to come after the flop you multiply your number of outs by four. With one card to come after the turn, you multiply your number of outs by two. This will give you a quick figure to work with. If you have a four-card flush after the flop you have nine outs. With two cards to come, you multiply the nine by four and you get 36 percent chance of making the flush. The chart shows the true odds at 35 percent. With one card to come, you multiply nine by two and get 18 percent. The chart shows that the true figure is 19.6. It is not completely accurate but it is pretty close, and it is an easy calculation to do in your head.

Chapter 35

Making Correct Decisions

What makes poker a game of skill and separates it from most other casino games is that your decisions matter. In poker your decision to bet, call, raise, or fold will have an affect on the outcome. Although your objective is to make money, your main concern when you play poker is to always make the correct decisions. You won't win every time you make the correct decision and you won't lose every time you make a bad decision. That's just part of the game but the player who makes the best decisions will win the most money in the long run. A winning player learns to be patient and not make rash decisions.

Patience makes way for confidence. You should learn to turn your attention outward. Rather than merely preparing for what you are going to do, take time to notice what the other players are doing. As you become more aware of the actions of others, you will be able to make more confident decisions of your own.

A player consistently making poor decisions will lose money. It has been said that in a low-limit game you will make more money from your opponents' bad decisions than you will from your good decisions alone. When your opponents make mistakes you must capitalize on them. Here are some mistakes that will be made by your opponents and hopefully not by you.

Playing Too Many Hands

Many players have made the decision to play, period. They will play any cards as long as they are involved in the hand. Once they are in a hand, they will continue to play to the end.

Playing Hands Out of Position

Many players will play weaker starting cards out of position. They leave themselves open to raises from players acting after them who have stronger hands.

Cold Calling Raises

Many players will routinely cold call raises before the flop with marginal hands. This is a costly mistake that will take its toll over a period of time.

Not Reading the Board

Some players don't read the board or read the board incorrectly. They will call a bet even though they are clearly beaten. I have seen players call a bet with a hand that is lower than the board cards. If a bet is made and your hand can't beat the board cards you must fold.

Checking Instead of Betting

Unless you have a very strong or unbeatable hand, you should bet after the flop. Too many times a player with a legitimate hand will check instead of betting. This allows any player who has a drawing hand to receive a free card, which could make a hand that will beat you.

Betting Instead of Checking

There will be situations when it will be better for you to check than to bet. If you have a drawing hand you want to see the next card as cheaply as possible. If you bet, you may be raised and it will cost you two bets. If you check, your opponent may check and you will receive a free card.

Folding the Winning Hand

This can prove to be the most costly mistake you can make. Sometimes it will be clear that you are beaten and you should muck your hand instead of making a crying call. If, however, you have stayed in the hand to the very end and the pot is extremely large you should call if there is a chance you may have the wining hand. If there is $100 in the pot and it will cost you $6 to call, you are getting over 16-to-1 odds for your bet.

Some Other Decisions

These are a few of the mistakes you may encounter during a game. There will be some decisions that you make that will affect you before you even sit down to play.

When you get to the casino you have to decide what game you want to play. The casino may offer several low limit games. You might be able to chose a $2/$4, $3/$6 or $4/$8 game. If you are a new player you may feel more comfortable in a $2/$4 game. Your bankroll may also be a consideration in your choice of a game. If this does not matter you should take a few moments to look at the games and the players.

Ideally you would like to play in a loose passive game that has a full table with many players participating in each hand. This should be more profitable than sitting at a half empty table of rock solid tight players.

Are You Prepared?

The most important decision you will make is one before you even leave your house. It is your decision whether or not to go play poker. If you are not prepared to play your best game, and devote your full attention to your play then you should stay home. Your attitude and frame of mind can and will affect your decisions at the table.

If you are upset or having a bad day, you may not be able to concentrate on the game. You should never play if you are tired or fatigued. As much as we all like to think that we can play under any circumstances, the truth is that no one plays their best game every time they sit down. It doesn't take much to throw off your game. If you are not totally prepared before you leave for the casino then it is best to wait for another night. I have had situations where I would debate whether or not I wanted to drive the distance to play for a few

hours. In each of the instances when I was undecided and then ultimately chose to go play, I had a losing session. Now, if there is any
doubt at all, I just stay home and wait for another day.

Chapter 36

We Are Not Fortune Tellers

Every day we are faced with making decisions. It doesn't matter if we are playing poker or going about our daily routine. We don't know the outcomes of our decisions until after the fact because, unfortunately, we are not fortunetellers. We don't have access to a crystal ball that will enable us to look into the future. Therefore the outcomes of our decisions don't always work out the way we had hoped they would. We also are victims of "selective amnesia." We tend to remember all the times a different decision could have brought about a favorable outcome, but forget about the times that our choice was correct. Here are a couple of common examples that have probably happened to you.

You look at your starting hand that consists of two little cards of the same suit. You toss it in the muck and sure enough the flop brings three more cards of the same suit. You lament that you would have had a flush if you had stayed in. The fact is you made the right decision. You forget about all the times the flop would have brought garbage and you would have lost to the player with a better hand.

Another time is when you are under the gun, and fold a small pair, only to see that you would have made a set if you stayed in. Again, you made the right decision. You had no way of knowing what the flop would bring. There is no reason in the world to start second-guessing yourself when you make the right decision. If you think such thoughts you should never vocalize them at the table.

Numerous times I have heard players complaining about the cards they mucked after they see the flop. They will make a comment about what they would have had if they stayed in. Here is an example:

The flop will be K-8-7. After the hand the player next to me will say, "I threw away King-8, I would have had two pairs." They then usually qualify the statement by saying, "Not that I would have played that hand."

Some players don't like to hear other players making statements like that. I am quite happy to let them tell me all about what hands they would have made if they knew what the flop would bring. By telling me about the hands that they threw away, I now have a better idea of the types of hands they will play. In this instance I know the player next to me is not going to play a single King with a weak kicker. This is good information to know.

Any time you make a comment at the table, you are revealing something to others about how you play your game. It is in your best interest to just make your best decision and then keep your mouth shut if you don't like the outcome.

There will be times when you will make a wrong decision while playing poker. Every player at one time or another has mucked a winning hand. It happens if you misread a player or the strength of his hand. There is nothing you can do to change the outcome. All you can do is continue with the game.

These are examples of decisions we make while playing Texas Hold'em, but there are other instances I see in my daily life as well.

Many of my friends and co-workers regularly trade stocks. It's not uncommon to hear someone lamenting that they sold a particular stock only to see it jump five points the next day. These same people complain that they should have sold earlier when they see a stock drop below the price they paid when it was originally purchased.

Have you ever cleaned out that garage or basement only to find that an item you look for the following week was thrown out? You lament that you should have saved that item for the future. The fact is it probably would have gone unused for the next ten years if you had saved it. You are not alone.

It's human nature to look at the outcome and lament on what would have happened if we made a different decision. You have no control over what will or will not happen. You DO have control over your decisions. You have to make your decision based on all the available facts that you have at your disposal and be confident that you are making the right choice. Sometimes this will not always bring about the desired outcome but you have to learn to accept the fact that you made the correct choice and then move on. They always say hindsight is 20-20.

We are only human. Sometimes we make a wrong decision. When this happens we need only ask ourselves if it can be corrected. If it can, we correct it. If it can't, we learn from it, we accept it, and we move on. Exhausting resources by worrying about past events that cannot be changed will serve no practical purpose. It will only make you crazy if you dwell on it, and if you let it bother you, it could affect your future decisions.

As human beings, we will all make right and wrong decisions at the poker table and in life. It is part of the learning and growing process. Anybody who has never made a mistake has never attempted anything new. It's how you handle the outcome of your decisions that really matters.

You are not a fortuneteller but you are an intelligent person. Make all your decisions in life based on the facts, as you know them. Understand that the outcome will not always be as you desired, but that's a fact of life we all must learn accept. Play your game and live your life to the best of your ability and be happy.

Chapter 37

Bad Beats

You look down at your starting hand and find the Ace of hearts and Ace of diamonds. You raise and get some action. The flop brings the 8 of clubs, Jack of hearts and 3 of diamonds. It's checked to you and you bet. The turn brings the Ten of clubs and again you bet and get callers. The river brings the Ace of clubs. This time the player in front of you bets. You call and he flips over the 4 and 6 of clubs for the flush. You have just suffered a bad beat.

A bad beat in poker is when you have a hand that is a favorite to win beaten by another hand. Most of the time the winning hand caught a miracle draw on the river. This is more common in low limit games because many players have the "any-two-cards-can-win" mentality. Many players will play any Ace and a few players will play any suited cards regardless of the rank. Some players are calling stations that will enter the pot with marginal or terrible hands and then call all the way to the river in hopes of making their draw. Occasionally they do make their hands and you suffer a bad beat. This is a fact that you must accept when playing in low limit games.

Bad beats are a normal part of poker that a good player learns to accept. As sure as the sun rises in the morning, you are going to occasionally get drawn out on the river, not so affectionately referred to as "drowning in the river." Some players complain about getting drawn out in the game but limit Texas Hold'em is a drawing game. If it weren't you would be playing two-card showdown. You will lose an occasional pot to a bad beat from these players but their bad play will lose to your solid play the majority of the time. In the long run, you will make money from players who constantly chase the inside straights or baby flushes.

Before you complain about a bad beat, take a look at your hand that was beaten. Did you belong in the hand to begin with? Suppose you played a hand like J-9 off suit from under the gun and made a straight on the flop. It gets down to the river and you lose to a baby flush. You complain that it was a bad beat. The truth is that you had no business playing that hand from under the gun to begin with.

There are also instances when your big hand will get beaten by a bigger hand. I call this a legitimate beat which, while rare, will happen occasionally. I once entered a hand with pocket Tens. The flop was three Aces giving me a full house. One player and I went all the way to the river. At the showdown she turned over a suited Ace and Queen. I have to admit I was not happy about it but things like that happen. I turned to the player and said, "Nice hand."

Some players get shaken up and go on tilt when they suffer a bad beat. You can't let it affect your play. If you get upset after suffering a bad beat, get up and walk away from the table for a hand. Cool down and then get back to your game. Part of winning poker is the ability to handle the psychological factors of the game.

Bad Beat Stories

Bad beats are like the weather. Everyone talks about it but nobody can do anything to change it. The weather is really a boring subject and so are bad beats. Everyone has suffered bad beats and by constantly talking about them you make yourself look like a whiner and a loser. If you want to talk about poker, why would you want to talk about your defeats? Whining about bad beats will not put fear into any of your opponents. Poker expert Mike Caro suggests you tell your opponents how lucky you have been and how the cards have been going your way. This will portray a winning image rather than a losing one. So the next time you get ready to tell a bad beat story, stop and ask yourself why would you want to tell a story about losing.

Chapter 38

Playing Your Best Game

Hold'em is more than just a card game. Whenever you are dealing with people you are also dealing with psychological factors. Your emotions as a player can have a large impact on your game. They say that winning can be simple. All you have to do is always play your best game. This is easier said than done for most of us. We can be our own worst enemies at times.

There are several factors that contribute to our own state of mind. Whenever you play, you should be well rested, alert and free from worrying about other problems in your life. If you bring these problems to the table with you, it can only interfere with playing your "A" game. Here is a tip that will save you money.

If you are getting ready to drive to the cardroom and you start to debate whether you really feel like playing, STAY HOME! Don't waste your time or your gas. You will more than likely have a losing session because your head is not in the game and you haven't even left home yet.

Playing your best, or "A" game, means that you are paying attention to the game at all times. You are aware of what hands the other players are playing. You are concentrating on reading the board. You know what the pot odds are when you call a bet. You also are playing premium starting hands.

You should also be confident of your own abilities. You don't have to be the best player in the world to win at Texas Hold'em. You just have to be better than the other players at the table. Some players can easily intimidate other players. This can happen if you find yourself over matched or in a ramming jamming game with a bunch of maniac players. You need to be aware of this. If, for any reason, you don't feel you can play your best game against the opponents at the table, or you think you are in over your head, then you should get out and find a different game.

Your game can also be affected by the play at the table. Some nights you will sit for hour after hour folding hand after hand while other players are winning with pure garbage. You will be tempted to start loosening up your standards for starting hands. Don't do it! When you do, you are getting away from your best game. If you are losing hand after hand, or are suffering bad beats, you could go on tilt.

Tilt

"Going on tilt" is the expression used when players become upset and lose control of their emotions. Consequently they start making poor decisions and play badly. A player on tilt will start to play any starting hands and call when he should not. If he has just suffered a bad beat, this could trigger him to go on tilt. He has lost money and is trying to make it back in one or two hands by playing overly aggressively with weak hands. His play becomes irrational. Like a child having a temper tantrum, he acts out in anger throwing chips in the pot trying to intimidate the other player. This will usually just lead to more losses.

Sometimes a player will get to the point where he just doesn't care how much money he has lost. Poker expert Mike Caro calls this crossing the threshold of pain. A player may be down a few hundred dollars and then figure what the heck does another hundred matter. It will matter a lot the next day to most players.

Players can go on tilt or steam when they direct anger at another player. This particular opponent may have beaten them out of a hand and they are now on a vendetta to get that person. They will raise and re-raise in hope of beating this player and getting their money back. This usually will backfire.

Players on tilt present a profitable situation for those at the table with a cool head. Often you will make money from one of these players. They will be throwing money around and it is up to you to catch it. Some may argue that its wrong to kick someone when he's down, but a player on tilt is fair game in a casino poker game. Just make sure it is not you.

Controlling Your Emotions

In his book, *Shut Up and Deal*, Jessie May says, "Poker is a combination of luck and skill. People think mastering the skill part is hard, but they're wrong. The trick to poker is mastering the luck."

It is critical that you learn to keep your emotions in check when you play. Every player is going to suffer bad beats and losing hands. It's the luck of the draw and bad players do get lucky at times. It is the player who can remain calm in the face of adversity who will be the ultimate winner in the long run. All the poker experts advise learning how to play "tilt free" poker. Most of the time it is more than one incident that will set a player off. I think most of us know when we start to feel our emotions building up.

There are several things you can do when you feel you are on the verge of losing control. The first thing to do is take a deep breath. Breathing gets more oxygen to the brain and will help clear up your thinking. It is the first thing you are taught if you have ever tried any form of meditation or deep relaxation exercises. It is very simple and can be done right at the poker table without being too noticeable.

1. Take in a deep breath through your nose. Count to four as you are doing this filling your lower diaphragm.
2. Hold your breath while counting to four again.
3. Slowly exhale through your mouth.
4. Repeat this four times.

If deep breathing does not help sooth you, get up and leave the table for a few minutes. Take a walk to the rest room. If the walk does not calm you down try washing your face and hands. A little cool water will help cool off the hot temper that you are feeling.

After taking a break, if you find that you are still not in control of your emotions, then you have no choice but to leave the game. If the cause of your aggravation is one particular player then you can switch tables if that is possible. If not, quit playing altogether. It is better to call it a night then to risk going on tilt.

Calm Conditioning

I have found a large number of poker players who regularly practice some sort of meditation or conditioning to help keep them calm and mentally alert in the game. They are not the only ones.

We have all had times when we have experienced peak performance. Athletes call it being "In the Zone,"; Zen Masters call it "Being as One"; others call it "Experiencing Flow." It is that time when all outside distractions are blocked out and our concentration is devoted solely to the task at hand. It can happen in our everyday work, when we play a game, read a book, see a movie, or play poker. When this happens, we are totally unaware of outside forces and time seems to speed by. In my first tournament win I actually was so much in the zone I was unaware when I actually had taken over as chip leader. My total concentration was on the game. This was not the first time I had been in the zone and I later learned that with a little practice you can learn to trigger this state and enter the zone on command with the help of a post hypnotic anchor.

A friend and fellow gaming author introduced me to the work of late psychologist Steven Heller, who taught many people how to enter the zone to achieve peak performance. Further study led me to the work of others who use the same simple technique, which is a form of self-hypnosis and visualization. Here is how to do it.

1. Find a quiet place where you will be undisturbed. Sit in a chair or lie down and make yourself very comfortable.
2. Think of a time when you had one of your greatest achievements or a time when you were totally confident. This might be a night when you had your best win at the tables. In my case I use my first tournament win, when I was making all the right moves at the table. This will be your power image.
3. Now mentally visualize everything you felt and heard when your power image was taking place. Amplify the feelings and images in your mind. Make the sound louder and the picture brighter.

4. When you amplify your power image you will get a feeling of supreme confidence. You will feel a sudden burst of energy. When this happens, you squeeze your thumb and index finger together forming a circle. This becomes your physical anchor to this image. You can also repeat a name or phrase associated with this image as your squeeze your fingers together. I use the code phrase "concentrate."

5. Repeat this routine ten times visualizing your power image while bringing your fingers together and repeating your code phrase. This will reinforce the link between your fingers and the confident feeling.

6. Repeat this exercise once or twice a day. Eventually you will be able to trigger your confident feeling and peak performance any time you desire.

7. You can use this at the poker table if you suffer a bad beat or if you feel your concentration slipping away. You can also use this in your daily life, anytime you find yourself in a situation where you need to be confident when making decisions.

Chapter 39

Losing Streaks

Poker is a positive-expectation game. This means that a good player can expect to make money over the long run using skill to outplay other players. No player, regardless of how skillful he may be, will win every time. Any time you play a game with an element of luck involved, you will encounter fluctuations brought upon by the mere luck of the draw. The ebb and flow of positive and negative fluctuation is luck. The positive end of the spectrum is good luck and the negative end is bad luck.

Even a bad player can get "lucky" from time to time, winning hands by getting miracle flops or catching an improbably winning card on the river. Conversely a good player can suffer a string of bad luck causing him to lose.

All players at one time or another will experience a losing streak. When this happens we need to determine if the losing was brought about by bad play on our part or just on a negative fluctuation in the luck of the draw. When you start losing, the first thing to do is to look at your game a little more thoroughly. One thing is certain; a losing streak can affect us psychologically. It can wreak havoc with us emotionally, causing us to second guess and question our own abilities and our play.

If the losing streak is being caused by bad play you need to determine why and then take action to correct the situation. There are several things you should ask yourself first. Did you loosen your standards for starting hands? Are you misreading the board? Are you playing too aggressively? If you can honestly answer no to these questions, then it may be that you were just suffering a string of bad luck.

If your losses are being caused by a bad run of the cards, then it's time to batten down the hatches and weather the storm. One thing you can do to combat a losing streak is to tighten up your game a little more. Play only the very best hands and forgo some of the drawing hands that you might have been playing.

My results during my first year of play were well above the normal expectations. I knew that I was playing well, but I also realized that my results would probably even out as time progressed. What I did not realize was that part of this would come in the form of a long losing streak at the start of my second year of playing the game. I began with a small loss after a session where every hand I called with was second best. Straights were beaten by flushes and flushes were beaten by full houses. I attributed the loss to normal fluctuations of the cards and was not too concerned.

My next session brought about the same results as the previous session. I was playing once or twice a week and this continued for a six-week period. In the past I had a few losing sessions in a row, but nothing to compare with my present slump. By the fourth week, I was starting to question my own play and decided to sit down to take a closer look at exactly what I was doing differently.

I found that I had been playing more drawing hands than I had in the past. Even though I was getting correct odds to make the draws, I was not succeeding in my attempts. This contributed to my losing sessions. I also noted that I had been playing longer sessions. I resolved to tighten my standards and go back to the tight game plan I had used when I started playing, and shorten my sessions. My fifth week I broke even, and then posted a win during my sixth week. I had snapped the losing streak by getting back to basics.

I was able to get back to winning by making some adjustments in my play. There was nothing seriously wrong with my game. While I was not pleased with the losing streak, I actually think that it helped improve me as a player. Rather than losing confidence in myself, I was able to overcome the negative emotional impact of the streak by honestly analyzing my own game.

Chapter 40

Playing in a Cardroom

Playing casino poker is quite different from playing in a home game. There are certain procedures and protocols you will need to understand before you sit down to play. It's not difficult making the transition from the kitchen to the cardroom and you will find that playing poker in the casino has many advantages over a home game.

One of the biggest advantages to playing in the cardroom is the availability of games any day or time you want to play. You won't have to worry if one of your regular players can't make it for the weekly game. You also don't have to worry about time constraints. You can play for as long as you want.

In a cardroom, you will find many players that are just out for a good time and don't play the game very well. When you are playing at home, and you have a poor player who loses all the time, he usually gives up playing after a few sessions. In a cardroom when a loser busts out and leaves the table, there are other players waiting to get into the game.

There are some procedures you need to be aware of when you play in a casino. You don't just walk up to a table and sit down. When you enter the poker room you must sign in at the desk. You tell the host what game you are interested in playing. If there is an opening you will be seated immediately. If the table is full they will take your initials and call you when there is an opening. Some casinos have a large board where they will write your name or initials or they will write your name on a list. Either way you will be called when it is your turn.

When your name is called, the poker room host will show you to your table. In some rooms the host will ask you how much you would like to buy in for and get you your chips when you are seated. At other casinos you will purchase the chips from the dealer when you sit down. You are allowed to bring chips from other games. All games have a minimum buy-in, which for most low-limit games is usually $30.

Posting

In many casinos a new player sitting down at the table has to post a bet equal to the big blind if he wishes to be dealt into the next hand. This is not mandatory and you may elect to wait until it is your turn to be the big blind before you enter the game. Waiting has a few advantages. It will give you time to observe your competition and determine the type of players at your table; notice the quality of starting hands being played and who is playing them. Is the table tight or lose? Observing the table while you wait will give you an insight about your competition. Waiting will also give you a few minutes to settle in and get your mind emotionally prepared for the game. If you can't get immediate seating when you sign in and find yourself on the waiting list for a game, it is advisable to watch the game in progress. Then when you do get a seat at the table you can post right away as you will already have a feel for the table. (See Railbirding.)

Taking a Break

Sooner or later you will need to take a break. You can get up and leave the table to go to the bathroom, stretch your legs, or take a break for any other reason. What you can't do is take your chips with you if you plan on returning to the game. The chips must stay on the table. The dealer will deal you out of the hand while you are away from your seat. If you do not miss any blinds it will not cost you any money while you are away from the table, as you want be involved in any hands. If you are gone from the table and miss your blinds, a button will be put in front of your chips showing that you have missed a blind. When you return from your break you will have to make up one big and one small blind if you have missed them both while you were gone. You can post it right away or wait until it is your turn to be the big blind again. The money for the small blind you missed will be put in the pot and the money for the big blind will act as a live bet. Even if you missed more than one big and small blind, you will only be required to make up one of each in most cardrooms.

I used to try and take my breaks after it was my turn to act as the blinds. I noticed one problem with this. I was always leaving the table when I was in late position giving up the advantage that acting later gave me. I discovered that if I had to leave the table and would miss more than a couple hands, I could actually turn this to an advantage. Instead of taking a break after the blind, I leave the table one hand before I am the big blind when I am going to be under the gun. Since this is the worst position, where you have to act first I don't mind missing this hand. I then return to the table after the dealer button has passed me. I post my big blind and I am now in the hand in late position with the option to check or raise when it is my turn. After the flop, I am second-to-last to act, putting me in extremely good position. Granted I have to forfeit my small blind, but most of the time I fold these if I don't have a playable hand. For the price of the small blind I have bought myself excellent position.

Most of the cardrooms I have played in are fairly liberal about the amount of time you can be away from the table. I think most of them are too liberal. If you are away from the table when there is a dealer change you are given an absent button. Every time a new dealer comes on board you get another one. If you are gone and get three absent buttons, they pick up your chips and give your seat to another player. Dealers change about every twenty minutes in the rooms where I play, which means a player can be away from the table for a full hour before losing his seat. I think this is very unfair to the players on the waiting list. It is also not fair to the players who then have to play short-handed. I have sat in on some games when two or three players are gone from the table at the same time.

One time a player returned to the table just as they were about to pick up his chips. One player asked him where he was and he told them he had gone to dinner. I asked him why he didn't just leave the game and come back after dinner. He glared at me and said he didn't want to lose his seat and have to be put on the waiting list. Three hands later, he picked up his chips and left. Some people have no consideration for others. If you think you are going to be gone for an extended period of time, give up your seat to a player on the waiting list. Remember, the shoe could be on the other foot some day.

Changing Seats

When you are first seated at a table you may not have a choice of seats unless it is a new game. This does not mean you can't change your seat once you are in the game. If a player is leaving the table, you can request his seat by telling the dealer as soon as you see him get ready to go. The main reason to change seats is to get the weaker players to your left and the aggressive players to your right. If you have a player who raises a lot you want that person sitting on your right. That way, if he raises, you can fold all but your stronger hands. If that person is sitting on your left, you may call with a borderline hand only to find that it will cost you a raise as well. Conversely you would like to have the weaker player on your left. A weaker player is predictable and, if he is also a calling station, you can profit from raising and knowing that he will call you.

Changing Tables/Must Move

Game selection is very important. You will find that some games are more profitable than others. You may sit down and find that everyone is so tight that you can't make any money. At other times, you may find yourself at a table with players more skilled than you. If you take a seat at a low-limit table and see all the regulars who usually play in the $30/$60 game killing time until their game opens up, you may not want to play there. Some cardrooms will have more than one game going at the limit you want to play. If, for any reason, you find you don't like the game at the table where you are seated, you can request a table change from the floor person. In some places you may be moved to a different table even if you like the game you are in. This happens when a cardroom opens up a must-move table.

The first table that opens at a particular limit is the main game. If you walk in the cardroom and want to play $3/$6 Hold'em, and there is only one game going on, you will be put on the waiting list. If there are enough players on the waiting list the cardroom may open up a new $3/$6 game. They will designate this a must-move game. They want to accommodate as many players as they can but they also want to keep the main game full. Therefore if a seat becomes open at the main table they will take a player from the must-move table. The players will be determined by the order in which they were seated at the must move table. The first player seated will be the first one to move to the main game.

If it's later in the evening, players will slowly trickle to the main game and the must move game will shut down. If it is earlier in the day, a new must-move table may open and the present one will become a permanent game. There have been times when I played at a must-move table that was very profitable only to have to move to the main game and found it was not to my liking. Unfortunately, the rules say you must move. If you don't want to move, your only other option is to take a break and then come back in to the cardroom and get put on the waiting list.

Game Selection

In some cardrooms there will be several games being played at the same limit. When you have a choice, you should pick a game that you think will be profitable for you. A game filled with rocks, who only bet when they have the nuts, will not be as profitable as a game with one or two calling stations. You should evaluate the skill level of the players in a game and determine where you fit in. If you feel that you are outmatched by the players at one table, you should look for a different game. Game selection will be a big factor in winning.

Comps

The word comp is short for complimentary. Comps are freebies that the casino gives to its customers as a reward for their business. It is a way to promote good will and to entice player loyalty to the establishment. Some cardrooms give you credit for your play in the form of comps. You may get free rooms, meals, an entry into a free roll tournament or points on a player's card that can be spent in shops or restaurants. Some casino poker rooms require you to join the casino's player's club and use that card as means of keeping track of your comps. At the Tropicana in Atlantic City, the poker room issues a separate Poker Club card to the players. Always ask at the desk when you sign in if the cardroom offers any comps to poker players. Anything that you get for free is just an added bonus to you.

Chapter 41

Table Stakes

We have all seen the Western movies where the tough desperados in black and the good guy in white sit around the poker table in the local saloon. At one point the hero will shove his stack of chips in the pot and say, "I don't think you have enough to cover this cowboy!"

At that point the bad guy, who just swindled the beautiful heroine out of her ranch, will whip out the deed to the property and say, "I think this will cover it." The hero proceeds to draw to an inside straight to beat the desperado. The girl gets the ranch the hero gets the girl, and the credits roll. It makes for great entertainment but has no bearing on reality in regards to casino poker.

In some kitchen-table games, a player can force out another player by betting more than his opponent has on the table. In other home games, you may allow someone to reach into their wallets or play "shy" to cover the bet. This does not happen in a cardroom.

Limit-Texas Hold'em has structured betting limits. You can not bet more than the limit designated for the game you are playing in. In $3/$6 Hold'em, the first two betting rounds are $3 and the last two rounds are $6. You are not allowed to bet or raise a different amount than these set limits. In most casinos there is a limit to the number of raises that can be made during each betting round. This is usually limited to three or four raises, unless the play becomes heads up between two players. In that case the number of raises becomes unlimited. If you are new to a particular cardroom, you should check to see what the rules are regarding the number of raises before you sit down

In casino poker you play for table stakes. This means that you bet only with the money that you have on the table. You're not allowed to go into your pocket for more money in the middle of a hand. If you run out of chips, you announce that you are "all in" and you will only be eligible for the money in the pot up to that point. Any additional bets made by other players will be put in a side pot. You will not be eligible for this side pot even if you have the best hand. This means that once a player is all in it is possible for a player with the second best hand to win some money from the remaining players in the hand.

You are allowed to buy more chips at any time between hands. You may also have money other than chips on the table that will be counted as part of your table stakes. Say you were to keep a $20 bill under your stack of chips. This would be counted as $20 on the table. In the middle of a hand, if you ran out of chips you would be able to place the money in for a bet and you would be given your change in chips. It counts because it was on the table before the hand was started. Some cardrooms permit chips only, so in such cases you will have to convert your cash when placing it on the table.

One of the most common questions asked about casino poker is how much you need to play. Most casinos have a minimum buy-in for each game. This is the minimum needed to sit at the table but it is usually a lot less than what you may actually need. In the $3/$6 Texas Hold'em game where I play, the buy-in is $30. This is only ten times the minimum bet of the first two betting rounds. This does not give you much of a cushion if you were to lose a hand or two. If you were to play a hand of Hold'em from start to finish, calling a bet on each round with no raises involved, it would cost you $18 if you lost the hand. I recommend that you start with about 15 to 20 times the big bet. In a $3/$6 Hold'em game I buy in for $100. This gives me enough money should I get involved in a big hand. There is nothing worse that running out of money and having to go "all in" when you have the winning hand. I learned this from experience one night while playing in a $4/$8 Texas Hold'em game at Foxwoods Casino.

I had bought in for $100, which is 12 times the large bet. I was not planning on playing too long as I was meeting some friends for dinner. I had a few second-best hands and my stack of chips was fading away. I had about $32 left when it was my turn to post the big blind. I posted my $4 big blind and was dealt a 7 and 9 of diamonds. Four players entered the pot and when it came to me, I "checked" my option to raise the pot. The flop was 7 of clubs and 8 and 10 of diamonds. I had a small pair as well as a four-card open-ended straight flush draw. The small blind had folded and I was the first to act. I bet $4 leaving me with $24. Two players called the bet and the flop brought a 2 of clubs, which was no help. I bet again and all but one player folded their hands. The last community card (the river) was the Jack of diamonds, giving me a straight flush. I bet $8 leaving me with only $8 left. The other player raised my bet immediately. I went all in with the last of my money. I had the "nuts" which is the best hand possible. Unfortunately I had no money left to re-raise the player. I was "all in." The other player turned over his Ace high flush. He was shocked when I showed my straight flush. He thought he had the best hand with his Ace high flush. He had not noticed the possibility that a straight flush could be made. As the dealer was pushing me the pot, the other player looked at me and said, "I am sure glad you were all in. I would have re-raised you until the cows came home!"

That lesson taught me to always back up my table stakes by putting more money on the table between hands when I get low on chips. Those types of hands don't come along too often, but when they do, you want to be able to capitalize on them. You can't do that if you are short on chips.

Bankroll Considerations

You will have winning and losing sessions. You need to have enough money in your poker bankroll to withstand the losing sessions. It has been advised that a good bankroll is one that is equal with 200–300 times the big bet. For $3/$6 Hold'em this would be $1,200–$1,800.

I have always advised anyone who visits a casino on a regular basis to maintain a separate bank account for his or her gambling activities. Money in that account should be earmarked for casino play only. That way you will always have the money needed when you head out for a session. You should never use money needed to cover the rent or other living expenses for any gaming activity.

I further advise that you set up a separate poker bankroll and keep this aside from money you may use for other casino games. Too many players win at the poker table and then go blow the winnings somewhere else in the casino. You should make it a habit to put your winnings back into your poker account. This will allow you to have the money when you decide to move up to higher limits of play. It is also a good exercise in discipline.

Chapter 42
Common Mistakes

Once seated in a game in the cardroom, you want to observe proper table etiquette and be careful not to make any of the common beginner mistakes. Here are a few of the common mistakes made by new players when they sit down to play casino poker for the first time. Actually some of them are made by experienced players as well.

1. Betting out of turn
You must wait until the player to your right acts. If you bet out of turn, this could give an unfair advantage to a player that did not act yet. If you raise out of turn, a player who might had called could fold. If you fold out of turn, you are giving an advantage to the player on your right who may have folded and now knows you won't raise.

2. Making a string raise
If you are going to raise you should announce "raise" when it is your turn. If you don't announce a raise, you must put the bet and the raise in at the same time. If you put in the bet and then go back to your stack for the raise, you can be called for a "string bet," which is not allowed, and your raise will not be honored.

3. Not knowing what the bet is
You have to know what the bet is when it is your turn. You must pay attention to the amount of the bet made by the first active player. Then you must be aware if the bet was raised.

4. Folding instead of checking

Sometimes if the player does not like the next card dealt, he will immediately fold when it is his turn. If you are first to act you can check. If everyone else checks, you get to see the next card for free. The same is true if everyone checks before it is your turn, you should also check instead of folding your cards. The free card may just make your hand. A fold instead of a check, essentially gives an advantage to the remaining players. There is now one fewer player in the hand that they need to worry about.

5. Throwing chips into the pot

Place your bet in front of you. This way the dealer sees that your bet is correct. He will scoop them into the pot. You don't throw them into the pot like you would at home.

6. Not protecting your cards

It is up to the players to protect their cards at all times. Place your hands or a chip on top of your cards. If another player's cards mix with yours when they throw in their cards, your hand will be declared dead. You will see some players bring a special weight or "Lucky Charm" to place over their pocket cards. It doesn't matter what you use as long as it is not so large as to interfere with the play of the game. Make sure to protect your cards until the pot is pushed to you. I once had the winning hand and the dealer pushed the pot to another player and swept my cards into the muck at the same time. I yelled that I had the winning hand. The floor was called and it was ruled that since my cards were in the discard pile I was not entitled to the pot.

7. Throwing a winning hand into the muck (discards)

The cards speak for themselves. Don't immediately throw in your cards if someone calls out a better hand. The dealer will declare the winner of the hand. Sometimes you may have a better hand than you thought you had. There is also the possibility that the player calling his winning hand has misread his own hand. Let the dealer declare the winner before mucking (throwing way) your hand.

8. Losing control of your emotions

Keep your emotions in check. The table is not the place for foul language or temper tantrums. It will not be tolerated. Besides it makes you look foolish. Veteran players as well as newcomers make this mistake. It is one that should not be made by anyone!

9. Playing too many hands

Many players crave the action. They feel that if they are not involved in the hand they aren't really playing the game. Successful players play fewer hands. It takes patience and discipline to wait until you have a proper starting hand. If you can practice these traits, you will be on your way to becoming a winning player.

10. Playing too long

Playing winning poker takes concentration. You must be aware of the game and people around you. If you play too long, you may get tired or even bored. This can cause you to make mistakes or play marginal hands. If you start to get tired leave the game. When I started playing, I would set time limits for each session. This helped to keep me focused and also helped me learn discipline by sticking to the limits I had set for myself.

Chapter 43

Types of Players

You will meet all types of players in the cardroom. Some will be young, some old. There are males and females and players of all races and nationalities. In this day of political correctness we are cautioned to refrain from any type of stereotyping of the individuals we meet. This is practical advice in and out of the cardroom. However, after playing Texas Hold'em for a while, you will find that most players will fall into a few common categories based on what hands they play and how they play them. Players can be loose or tight along with being passive or aggressive.

Loose Players

Loose players believe that any two cards can win. They have no set standard as to which hands they play and will try to play as many hands as possible. They want to be involved and, once they are in the hand, they are reluctant to fold. These are recreational players and gamblers. They come to play and play they shall. Since they are playing a lot of hands, they consequently will win quite a few pots. However, in the long run, their wins will not offset all their losses. Having a lot of loose players in the game can make for some really large pots.

Tight Players

Tight players are just the opposite of loose players. They are very selective about the hands they play. They will only play premium hands that will have the best chance of winning. They usually refrain from playing gapped drawing hands in favor of the large cards and pocket pairs. Tight players will win more money in low-limit games, as other players are less likely to notice that they are playing very few hands. In higher-limit games, or games with knowledgeable players, there will be more players folding when the tight player does bet.

Passive or Weak Players

Passive players like to check and call. They don't like to raise and they will play their hands without much conviction. They won't push their hands by raising, preferring instead to let other players dictate the action. Because a passive player will call raises and bets, you stand to make money from this player when you win. You also will lose less money when they have the better hand because they have not been raising you.

Aggressive Players

Aggressive players will play their hands strongly. They will raise when the opportunity presents itself. They like to control the action, preferring to bet or raise rather than check or call. They are not afraid to check raise or cap the betting to eliminate other players. Aggressive players can intimidate passive players and, at times, run all over them.

You can mix and match these categories and break the majority of players down into four basic groups.

Loose-Passive

This group is also known as the "calling station." They will play many hands but will not play them strongly. A calling station will cold-call two raises before the flop and stay until the river, looking for that miracle draw. Even if it is clear that they are beaten, they will sometimes call just to keep you "honest" or to see what you had. There are some downsides to the calling station. They are the ones who will inflict the worst bad beats on you because of the cards they are playing and the fact they are staying to the end. You have to accept this as a fact of life and be emotionally prepared when the bad beat comes along. In the long run, you will win more from these players than you will lose to them. You don't want to discourage them or drive them out of the game by berating them and criticizing the way they play. If you do get beat by a calling station tell them, "Nice Hand!" Encourage them to continue playing just the way that they are.

Loose-Aggressive

These players are also referred to as maniacs. They never saw a hand they couldn't raise with. They crave action and want as much of it as possible. They will play many hands and will be betting and raising at every opportunity. This is the player you want to have sitting on your right so you can fold your weaker hands when they go into action. The problem with the maniacs is that you never know what hand they are raising with. Under the gun, they could just as easily be raising with A2 as AA. These players will cause the biggest fluctuation in your bankroll. They also will contribute to some of your biggest wins.

Tight-Passive

Tight-passive players are sometimes referred to as rocks. They play only premium starting hands, but they don't play them strongly, opting to check and call, rather than bet, raise, or check-raise. When a rock makes a bet you can be sure he has a very strong hand. If you have been paying attention to the players in the game, you will be able to spot the rock at your table. Some players joke that you can tell rocks by looking at the cobwebs on their stack of chips. These players like to receive free cards until they make a strong hand. When you are in a game with a majority of tight players, you will see more checking going on than betting. Tight passive players can also be bluffed more easily than other players. If you are in late position with active players limping in and checking on the flop, you can probably steal the pot with any bet made on the turn. You will lose to the rock if you do not have a strong hand. They hardly ever bluff, so when you are raised by one of these players, you will save money by mucking your hand if you don't have anything near the nuts.

Tight-Aggressive

A tight aggressive player is a force to deal with. If this is not you, then it should be your role model. This is the type of player you want to be. If you are new to the game, or are trying to improve your present game, you must understand that it will take a little work and effort on your part before you get to where you want to be. It doesn't happen overnight, but you can start at your next session by being more selective in the hands you play. Before the flop you play solid starting hands. After the flop you are going to read the board and determine how your hand stacks up against the best possible hand that can be made from the board.

If you decide to go on after the flop, you will play aggressively. A winning player is usually the one that initiates the action. If you are first to act, rather than checking, bet. If there is a bet before you, consider raising rather than calling. You should be well aware of the complete arsenal at your disposal including check-raising, slow playing, semi-bluffing, and how to gain a free card if necessary.

You should always be aware of the number of players involved in the hand. Was there a raise before the flop? If so who raised and what type of hands has that person been playing? You should also be aware of the pot odds and ask yourself if the odds justify calling a bet or raise. These are some of the questions that should cross your mind before you make your play. Winning players are leaders, not followers.

When I first started playing, I had no problem playing a tight game. I did discover that I was not being as aggressive as I should be. I made a conscious effort to change this. As I started playing more aggressively, I noticed a remarkable improvement in my game. The change came about as I developed more confidence in my own ability.

Foxes

Fox is a term mostly associated with tournament players or professional players. Foxes have the ability to play deceptively. They may appear to play loose but then change gears and tighten up their play at any given time. They are masters at the art of deception and if you come across one at a table, you may find yourself being out played. These players have excellent results in higher-limit games, but some of their fancy plays will be lost on most low-limit players who don't pay attention to the play of others. If you plan to move up to the higher limit games, you will have to learn to incorporate some of the Fox's traits into your game. Unlike the low-limit games where "Tight Is Right," your opponents at the higher level will pick up on your tight play and not give you much action.

Types of Games

As you can probably figure out, the type of game that you are in will be dependent upon the types of players sitting at the table. Most of the time you will have a mixture of players but, more than likely, you will find yourself with the majority of players having the same style.

No Fold'em Hold'em

This is the term given to games that contain a large number of calling stations. The game is usually very loose with a lot of players seeing the flop and many of them calling all the way to the river. This type of game is also called "Showdown Poker" because you will have to "show down" the best hand at the end. There is absolutely no time in this game when it will be correct to try a bluff. It just won't work. You can play your normal style (tight-aggressive) in this game. You can raise knowing that you will be called. You just have to make sure you will be showing down the best hand.

Wild Games

In wild games you will have a large majority of loose aggressive players. They will want to cap the betting before the flop and continue betting after the flop. This type of game can produce big fluctuations in your bankroll if you play your normal style. You will have to tighten up your game even more than normal and wait for the big solid hands to play. You may not be playing many hands, but the ones you do win will be huge. It has been my experience that most of the wild games I have been in consisted of mostly younger males who are out having a good time and showing off a little macho bravado at the tables. If this type of game makes you feel uncomfortable then you should find another game.

I experienced one of my biggest wins in a wild game. I had gotten to the casino in the wee hours of the morning. I sat down and it did not take me long to determine that most of these guys had been drinking and playing most of the night. Four of the players in the game were trying to out-do each other. They were calling "raise" before the dealer could flop or turn the cards. The dealer had to remind them to act in turn. I was able to get a seat with all of them on my right. I patiently waited for a premium hand to play. My patience paid off as I was dealt pocket Aces during one hand and the flop of A-2-2 gave me the nut full house. I did not even have to worry about betting because the pot was capped before it was my turn to act. These four guys capped each betting round right to the river. The highest hand among them belonged to one player who had the fourth Ace for two pairs. They were stunned when I showed my full house.

Tight Games

If you are in a game with many tight players you will see much smaller pots, as there will be fewer players involved in each hand. They will be very selective about the hands they play and will do a lot of checking, looking for a free card if they are on a draw. Usually a bet will drive them out in this situation. If the game is passive as well as tight, you may be able to loosen up a little since you will be seeing the flop fairly cheaply. If there is ever a correct time to bluff in low-limit Hold'em, it will happen when you are in an extremely tight passive game. If you attempt a bluff in a tight game and are called or raised, you should immediately give it up. Many of the tight games I have played in have been in the afternoon at local casinos. The players were older and many of them were retired. Not all of these tight games were passive. I have met some of the toughest players in these games.

Study the Players

The only way you will be able to determine the types of players you are up against is by studying them during the game. You should spend your time observing the other players when you are not involved in the hand. Many players will sit in a game for hours and, if you asked them any specifics about their opponents, they would not be able to give you an answer. I make it a point to watch one or two players per hand. Any player who raises gets my attention. If he is in the hand until the end, I want to know exactly what hand he raised with. This will help me determine if he is a solid aggressive player, or a loose maniac trying to get some action. It won't be too hard to determine who is playing tight and who is playing loose. Although I mentioned two examples of age when I talked about younger males playing loose and older people playing tight you can't rely on such generalities to judge other players.

During my third session of Hold'em, I met a women named Lois who is a regular at the casino where I do a lot of my playing. I sat next to her at the table and noticed she was using a key chain from Las Vegas as a weight to protect her cards. We struck up a friendly conversation about different casinos in Las Vegas and then talked about the game of Hold'em. We have played at the same table many times since. Lois is an older woman who reminded me a lot of my grandmother. She always has a bag of candy with her, which she generously shares with other players, and is one of the friendliest persons I have yet to meet in the casino. She is also one of the sharpest low-limit players; she consistently wins when she plays. Anyone looking at her probably would not think that she would be a force to reckon with at the tables.

Table Image

Developing a table image is the art of deception, which will help confuse your opponents about the type of player that you are. You may want to give the appearance of being loose or tight, but then mix it up and change gears. This is important in higher-limit games, but all of this is lost on the majority of opponents at the lower-limits. Author Lou Krieger suggests adopting a style that is close to your natural personality. If you are somewhat conservative, you may find it difficult to sustain an act where you try to come across as a maniac. If you play in the same cardroom and play against some of the same players, it will be easier to adopt an image closer to your real personality. If you establish a tight image it is easy to occasionally play a little looser and deceive other players who are used to your style. I have also found that you can appear loose even when you are playing a tight game. Many loose players are happy go lucky and will talk and chat with fellow players. You can do this and still keep one eye on the game. Your outward appearance will make you seem loose, while you covertly study your opponents and pay attention to the game.

Many players wear a baseball cap or sunglasses to hide their eyes so they will not give off any tells that can be picked up by other players. This is a good idea, especially in tournaments, and it is quite normal to do one or the other. However, some players think that doing both will give them the sinister impression that will strike fear in other players. When a player sits down at a $2/$4 or $3/$6 Hold'em game dressed like the "Unabomber" complete with hat, sunglasses, and hood, it has the opposite effect than the one he is trying to convey. It's best to pick one or the other.

Chapter 44

Tells

A tell is a mannerism or physical movement that can give you an indication of the strength of an opponent's hand or tell you if the player is bluffing. It can be a voluntary movement to try to deceive you or it can be an involuntary reaction to the cards. The term tell is short for "a telltale sign." If you can learn to spot tells, you will be able to win some hands just by reading another player. Once you master the basics of the game, and are playing winning poker, you can learn to read your opponents and increase your profits. Tells are the body language of the poker table. Some tells are fairly obvious while others can be subtler.

Acts Weak When Strong

One of the universal tells you will discover is that most players will act strong when they are weak and act weak when they are strong. Players who look sad or shrug when placing bets in the pot usually have a very strong hand. They will sometimes verbalize this by saying in a weak voice, "Oh, all right I'll call." They may use some other expression, but anytime they act reluctant to call, you can be certain that they have a strong hand. A player making a loud, forceful bet with much fanfare usually does not have a strong hand.

Where Are They Looking?

A player staring right at you is daring you to call them. They are try-ing to intimidate you into folding by daring you to call their bet. A player looking away from you, trying to seem uninterested, usually has a strong hand. That player wants you to call and is trying to seem nonchalant about his hand.

Suddenly Paying Attention

I mentioned this tell earlier in the book when I wrote about starting hands, but it should be repeated here. When a player who is reading or watching TV looks at the cards dealt to him and sets down the magazine or directs his attention to the game, then he has a playable hand.

Staring at the Flop

After the flop cards are turned up on the board, a player staring at the flop usually was not helped by it. A player who sees the flop and immediately looks away or glances down at his chips has made a hand.

The No Flush Tell

If a player looks at his pocket cards when three cards of the same suit flop, he usually doesn't have a flush. Chances are he has one card of that suit and he wants to see the value of the suited card.

Shaking Hands

If a player's hands are shaking when he makes his bet, you can be sure he has have a very strong hand. This is an involuntary tell that is not an act. I know this from experience. When I won my first tour-nament I had so much adrenaline pumping through my body that I found myself shaking when I made a big hand. I knew I was doing it but had difficulty trying to control it. One observer actually men-tioned this to me after the match was over.

Breathing

You can tell the strength of a player's hand by noticing changes in his breathing. This is another involuntary tell. A player who starts breathing rapidly after seeing the next card has a strong hand. If you are close to this player you may actually hear him breathing. On the other hand, if a player is holding his breath waiting for you to act, then he is usually bluffing.

Counter Tells

Now that you know a few of the common tells, you can work on your own game to make sure you are not sending out these tells to other players. You can also work on counter tells to send just the opposite signal. One way you can do this is by always acting strong when you are strong and acting weak when you are weak. This will throw off some of the players who may be looking for the opposite sign.

I like to send off a counter tell when I make a flush on the flop. I will purposely look at my pocket cards to give the impression that I did not make the flush. I will then smooth-call a bet on the flop and raise on the turn.

Be on the Lookout

These are just a few of the tells you may see at the table. There has been a lot written about tells, as they deal with the psychological aspect of the game. Poker expert Mike Caro has written books and produced videotapes about tells. It is part of the game you will want to study more about as you strive to improve. Keep in mind that you will not be able to spot any tells if you are not paying attention to the other players. You must be looking for tells in order to spot them and this means keeping your focus on the game all the time. When you are not involved in a hand you can devote more attention to studying the other players in hopes of spotting a tell or two.

Control Yourself

While it is important to look for tells from other players, it is more important to not give off any tells of your own. You should concentrate on controlling your own emotions and expressions so you don't give your opponents any clues about your hand. Have a trusted friend watch your play and let you know if he can detect any tells you may have.

Chapter 45

Cheating and Collusion

If everyone were as honest as you and I, we would not have to worry about cheating when we played poker. The fact is that the majority of players are honest and ethical. However, when money is involved there will always be someone looking for an angle to get more than what rightfully belongs to them. Unfortunately this is a fact of life and we must be aware of the possibility and take measures to ensure that it does not happen to us when we play.

In cardrooms where a dealer is supplied, you don't have to worry about being dealt seconds or some other form of manipulation on the part of the dealer to cheat you. What you do have to be concerned about are the other players at the table. There is cheating that can take place by a single person trying to gain an advantage over you. There is also collusion that takes place amongst two or more players.

The most common form of cheating by a single player is when the person sitting next to you tries to look at your hole cards. If he can see what you have, he has a big advantage over you, as he can fold a losing hand or raise if he has you beat. Fortunately, this is the simplest form of cheating to guard against. All you have to do is cover your cards with both your hands as you look at them for the first time. Practice looking at your cards while covering them. Have a friend sit next to you and try to peak at them. Make sure you are looking at your cards in a way so they cannot be seen by another player.

After looking at your cards, memorize them and don't look again. At this point when you put them back down, you want to cover them with an object such as a couple of chips or coins. Some players bring some sort of lucky charm to the table for this purpose. The reason you cover your cards is to protect them from getting mixed into the discards or getting fouled by another player's cards. This is another form of cheating that occurs when a player purposely throws his cards into yours. If your cards are not protected, they can be declared dead if the other player's cards touch them.

Sometimes a player will declare a hand that he does not have in hopes that you will throw your cards into the muck and the player will then win by default. As an example, suppose you have the winning pair. A player announces that he has a flush. You throw your cards into the muck and then see that this player only has a four flush. He might say something along the lines of, "Gee, I thought I had a flush." Since you threw your cards away, he wins. Always hold onto your cards until the winner is determined. Don't muck your cards just because a player announces that he has you beat.

Another move a player might use to gain information is to make a move toward the pot with chips in his hands pretending to bet only to pull it back once he sees what your intentions are. If he has a weak hand, and sees you reaching for your chips to bet, he might then check or fold. If he has a strong hand and knows you are going to bet, he now has the perfect opportunity to check-raise you. The way to combat this is to always wait a few seconds until the player has completed his action before you make your play.

There is a line from the movie *Rounders* that states: "If you can't spot the sucker in your first half hour at the table then you are the sucker!"

This line deals with the issue of collusion when two or more players in the game secretly conspire to cheat you. Players may secretly signal their hands to each other. They may start raising every time the mark or target enters the hand. They will either try to drive that player out after he has bet or enough of them will stay in the hand until the end with the likelihood of one of them drawing out the targeted player. When the player turns over his hand, if one of them has him beat, he will show his cards and the rest will quietly muck their cards without showing what they were raising or calling with.

When I first started playing, I had heard stories about collusion but did not really believe that this would happen in a low limit game in a casino cardroom. After experiencing it first hand, I am now on the lookout whenever I play.

I entered one of the smaller cardrooms on the Strip in Las Vegas. There was a $3/$6 game going on and I waited for a seat to open. The game seemed fairly normal as I watched from the rail. I did notice that most of the players in this game knew each other by the conversation that was going on at the table. I finally got a seat and sat down. I said hello to my fellow players and received a few grunts in response.

This particular casino allows a maximum of four raises during each betting round. On the third hand I was dealt Ah-Jd and limped in from middle position. The player to my left immediately raised the pot. The player to his left re-raised, as did two other players at the table. It was capped when it got back to me costing me an additional $12 to see the flop.

The flop brought Jc-Js-2c and I bet my trips and the betting was capped again. The turn was 4h and the same betting and raising took place. The river brought a third club on board. I checked and the other four players bet and raised. I figured that I was probably beat but the pot was huge so I called. Sure enough one player turned over T-4 of clubs and the others just threw their cards in face down. It would be easy to write this off as a bad beat, but I had been watching this game while waiting for a seat and had noticed this player had been playing solid starting hands. I was surprised that he would play a Ten and a 4 in a raised pot from middle position. I had also noticed that there was not much raising going on before I sat down.

Things returned to normal as I folded the next few hands. When I was the big and small blind the betting was again capped before it got to me. Finally, I was on the button and called with a playable but not great hand. The big blind raised me and this was re-raised by a player who had previously limped in. This time I folded getting out for $3. I then picked up my chips and left the table. It was so obvious what was being done that I had no desire to stick around any longer. It did not take me the full half-hour to determine who the sucker was in this game.

Looking back I probably should have made a comment to the floor person when I left but I was not sure if anything would have been done, as most of these guys seemed to be regulars. My advice to anyone who thinks there is collusion going on is to leave the table as quickly as possible. There is no reason to hang around even if you only suspect you might be getting cheated.

Online Poker

Playing poker online is gaining in popularity and many players log on each day to play for real money. I have played and practiced online but am still skeptical about playing for any large amount of money in games on the Internet. First let me say that there are many reputable sites offering online poker and I have been assured that they do everything in their power to make sure these games are as honest as they can be.

One operator of an online poker site told me that they have more control over detecting suspected collusion. He said all the hands are recorded and they can go back and look at the play of all the players and see exactly what hands players were holding when any suspect activity occurred. This is fine for detecting instances of players overrunning another player with raises but there are other forms of cheating that may go undetected.

There are numerous ways that players online can communicate with each other. Internet Relay Chat, ICQ, instant messaging, and telephones can all be used to relay information to each other. Several players in a game communicating with each other could share what cards they held making it easier to figure out what hand the other player may have by the cards he can't hold. With multiple phone lines and laptop computers you could even have several players sitting next to each other in the same room while they play.

In a cardroom it is one player to a hand. You can't turn around and ask a spectator how to play a particular hand. This is not the case online. I know for a fact that during some online tournaments some players will get together and play as a group. One player will actually play in the tournament while four or five of his advisors will be with him online offering advice as to the best play via instant messaging. A player can even have his advisors sitting next to him in the same room while he plays.

Finally, if you do play online, make sure you chose an established site with a good reputation. There have been a few instances where a site simply went out of business and disappeared along with all the players' money.

Although the majority of players, cardrooms, and online sites are honest, you still have to be on your guard whenever your money is involved.

Chapter 46
Money Management

Since most casino games have a negative expectation, players are advised to set a win goal and stop loss. This ensures than that they will not go broke during any given session and will hopefully not give back all the profits if they do win. Some argue that the concept of money management is nothing more than smoke and mirrors because if you play a game with a negative expectation you will lose in the long run.

I'll admit that in my weekly gaming column and magazine articles that I do recommend setting loss limits and win goals for casino players. The win goal is on a sliding scale and increases as the winning continues. This way players can continue to win without having to stop at predetermined figure. The stop loss is to ensure that they do not go broke too quickly and is also on a sliding scale if they have been winning. This is to ensure that they walk away with some of the money they have won. Again you can argue the merits of such a system but the main reason why I advocate money management is discipline. It takes discipline to be a winner at any casino game. This is especially true in poker where you have to wait for the right starting hands.

Poker has a positive expectation for good players and most of the pros and experts will tell you that any money management system is worthless. Poker is one big game with a few interruptions to eat, sleep, and work between hands. It doesn't matter if you quit when you are ahead or losing, as you will be coming back to the game eventually. They say that if the game is good it doesn't matter if you are down because you will win money back in the long run if you are a good player. I agree with this up to a point. I still think that you should have some sort of stop loss for each session.

I advocate a stop loss for psychological reasons. If you are losing and suffering bad beats or just being dealt rag hand after rag hand, there will come a point where this will start affecting your mental game. When this happens, you are no longer able to play your best game. You may find yourself making poor decisions or playing hands that are below your standards. When this happens its time to quit.

I suggest that you buy in for a reasonable amount of money. In a $3/$6 game I will buy in for a minimum of $100 which is equal to 16 big bets. If I lose this, I will usually call it a night. If the majority of the loss came from losing only one big hand then I will evaluate the game and my own state of mind. I might take a break if I am going to continue playing.

Another factor I consider when deciding to quit is the length of time that I have been playing. When I first started playing, I found that I could not keep total concentration on the game for more than a couple hours. I then would limit my sessions to a certain time period and then quit whether I won, lost, or drew. Each of us has our own endurance level. Some people can play at peak performance for hours on end. Others might lose concentration after an hour. You have to decide what is best for you. One way to determine your performance level is to look at your logbook. Compare your win/loss record with your playing time and see if the amount of time you spend at the table is having an effect on the outcome of your play.

Chapter 47

Keeping a Log

One of the most informative reference books you will read about poker will be written by you. It is your logbook where you will record the results of all of you poker sessions. If you are serious about your game it is imperative that you keep a log. Only by keeping records will you be able to tell if you are a winning player or not.

Many players don't feel that it is necessary to keep records. If you ask these same players if they are winners, they will usually answer in the affirmative. The truth is that without records, there is no way to be certain. Many players have selective memories. They tend to remember the big wins and will tell you that they occasionally lose "a little." It is possible that these little losses, when added together will offset the winning sessions that they remember. The only way to be sure if you are truly a winner is through honest and meticulous record keeping.

Keeping records is a matter of being truthful with yourself. Your log is your own personal record. If you fudge it, or put in false figures, you are defeating the purpose of keeping the log. If you aspire to be a winning player you need to know if your game has leaks so you can plug them and get back on a winning course.

You log does not have to be fancy. If you have a computer you can use a spreadsheet program to keep track of you sessions. You may want to print out a log sheet similar to the one at the end of this chapter and keep it in a notebook. There are poker diaries you can purchase, made specifically for players, which also contains some poker data and out charts. No matter what method you use there is some information that should be put in all logs.

Date and Location

Record the date and the cardroom where you played. You may find that you play better in certain locations than others. This could have to do with travel time or just the fact that you are more comfortable playing in certain locations. It could also be that the competition is easier in one place than another.

Limit

You may have several limits that you play. One casino may offer only $3/$6 games another could offer a $2/$4 or a $4/$8 game. Since your goal is to win at least one big bet per hour, you need to know what limits you are playing. You might find that you are more confident at the lowest level or you may do better against players at the higher limits. This will be one of the factors you evaluate when you look at your results.

Hours Played

You want to record the length of time that you play. This is one of the equations used in figuring your hourly win rate. It will also be important in evaluating your level of stamina and concentration. You may find that you get better results with shorter sessions than you do in marathon games.

Money Won or Lost

Record the money you won or lost for each session. This is easy to do. You know how much money you bought in for and you write down the difference at the end of the session.

Hourly Win/Loss

Figuring out you hourly win or loss rate is just a matter of simple math. You divide the amount of money you made or lost in a session by the number of hours that you played. If you played and won $28 after four hours of play your hourly win rate is $7 per hour (28 divided by 4 = 7).

Total Win/Loss

You should figure your hourly rate for each session. If you play more than one session during your visit to the casino or cardroom, then record each one as a separate entry. You can now add all your sessions together to get your total for the week, month, or year.

Fluctuation and Standard Deviation

It is only normal that you will have winning and losing sessions. This is a normal fluctuation that is measured by the standard deviation. The average wins for a good player is about one big bet per hour. In a $3/$6 game you can figure about $6 per hour as the estimated value or EV that you expect to earn. Some session you make more than $6 and some you make less. The difference between the actual amount won or lost and the $6 is the standard deviation. If you have large wins and then large losses your deviation will be high. You will need a big bankroll to handle the big swings. Your goal should be to cut down on the gap and bring your variance down to a small amount.

Additional Notes

Your log is your poker diary. You should write down any other information or events that occurred during the session. I printed my log on only the front side of the sheet that I keep in a notebook. On the back side I record any information that may help me in the future.

My Play

After each session I try to critique my own play as objectively as I can. If I made a loose call or stupid bet I would note my mistake in my log so I won't repeat it. I also make a note if I was too passive or too aggressive. Anything that can affect my future game will go into the log. Whether it's a great play I want to repeat in the future, or a situation where something caused me not to play my best game, it is written down. I found that when I write something down it has a much greater impact on me. Write down how you felt after the match. Did you play your best game? What contributed to the results you had during the session? Was the game loose or tight?

Other Players

One day I played against a Hobbit, a president, and Walter Cronkite. No, they weren't really sitting at my table, just people that made me think of these folks. One player was the spitting image of Richard Nixon and sitting next to him was a funny-looking guy who brought to mind Bilbo Baggins from *The Hobbit*. Joining us at the table was a fellow who looked like Cronkite. I can't always get the names of the people I play against so I often use some sort of association to help me remember them. I keep notes on different players I have met at the tables and I can identify them with the names from this association. I put these notes in my logbook so I can remember how they play or any tells I may have discovered that they have. I make a note if a certain player is a maniac, tight or a calling station? You can write down any information about them you think will come in handy when you play them again. Spending a few minutes making notes about players can reap big rewards the next time you face them.

Review Your Log

You should review your log to help analyze your play. If you have been losing try to figure out the reason why. Are you playing too long? Are you doing better at one limit than another? Are you having wide swings in your results? If you keep good notes you should be able to gain some insight into your own play when you study your log. As you grow and improve as a player you should be able to notice the difference and see the results by looking at your log.

Date	Casino	Limit	Win/Loss	Hours	W/L per hour	Total

Part Three

Learning the Game

Chapter 48
Training

Whatever you choose to do in life you will need knowledge to succeed. In order to gain that knowledge, you need to participate in some sort of training process. Unfortunately you can't learn by flipping a switch or swallowing a magic pill, but there are many ways you can choose to learn about your given area of interest. You obviously need formal education for some professions, but other subjects can be learned through home study, reading, on-the-job training, or spending some time at "The School of Hard Knocks."

No matter what you chose to learn about, you will need patience and discipline. Learning is an ongoing process that does not happen overnight. People who only learn the minimum about a given subject usually find themselves on a fast track to disaster. This was borne out in January 2000 when many people learned how to open an online brokerage account and suddenly considered themselves to be savvy investors. They started investing in the latest hot stock without regard to PE ratios or other financial indicators. Reality kicked in when the market took a downturn in April of that year and their financial gains turned into losses. The same thing happens in the casino and poker rooms.

I use the stock market analogy because playing poker is similar to investing in the stock market. You invest your money in the pot and you are looking for a return on that investment. When choosing a stock you are looking for solid companies that have a good business model and thus the best chance of returning a profit on your investment. In poker, you want to start with solid starting hands that have the best chance of winning you the pot. Many investors gamble on penny stocks. Occasionally, they will find one that makes a huge profit, but most of time they lose money in the long run on them. This can be compared with the poker player who constantly plays any two cards as a starting hand. Occasionally the player will get lucky and win a big pot, but this will not offset the losses from continually playing poor hands.

Many other skills and traits of a successful investor can be found in a winning poker player. A poker player must have the patience to wait for a strong starting hand and the investor must patiently wait for his investment to show a return. Discipline is needed to be able to refrain from jumping into speculative investments or playing marginal cards. It is also needed to be able to bail out when the investment goes bad, or fold the cards when the hand is beaten. Being properly capitalized is also required in both endeavors. Some good stocks are too expensive for your portfolio and some good poker games have limits higher than you can afford. Money management is a factor, as you don't want to invest all your money in one stock or risk your entire bankroll in one playing session.

To be successful in both poker and investing, you need knowledge. Investing and poker require making the correct decisions at the right time. You need an understanding of all the principles involved in order to achieve this.

Some players learn the basic mechanics of playing poker by reading a pamphlet or watching others play. Then they sit down at the table and jump into the game. Some of these players may get lucky for a while and consider themselves to be savvy poker players. You will see many of these types at the low-limit tables and some at higher limit games as well. Sooner or later reality kicks in for these players and their lucky winning sessions turn into losing sessions as they find themselves outplayed by more skillful players.

If you want to be successful, you need to learn a little more than just the basic play of the game. Successful poker players are constantly learning. Seasoned pros will tell you that they still learn something new with each session they play. Most successful players started with a strong foundation and built their game from there.

When I made the decision to learn Texas Hold'em, I wanted to make sure that the method I used would give me the best chance of success when I played in the casino. Since two of the most important traits necessary for winning in poker are patience and discipline. I decided to practice both of these as I learned the game. I did this by setting a target date for my first match that was a little more than a month away from the day I started to learn the game. By choosing to do this, I would force myself to be patient and not hurry into a game before I was ready. I set aside a minimum of an hour a day for study and practice and disciplined myself to stick to my schedule.

It's human nature to want to jump into the action of playing poker, and some may feel that the guidelines I set for myself were a little obsessive. I disagree. I plan to play winning poker for years to come. I felt that spending a month or so learning the basics of the game and building a strong foundation was a minimum investment for the rewards I plan to collect in the future. Furthermore, this was not some boring subject that I was trying to sift through. I was learning to play Texas Hold'em, which I soon discovered is one of the most exciting games I have ever played. My approach to learning the game was not only educational, but also fun. When I finally sat down at the poker table for the first time I found that it was also profitable.

In the beginning of this book I told you that I usually recommend three essential items to anyone wishing to learn a casino game. They are a book, software program, and videotape. My training got under way with these items I had purchased from the Gambler's Book Shop. I soon discovered that I would need to do just a little bit more to make myself ready to play Texas Hold'em. Since poker is more complex than other casino games, it would require more than reading a single book and playing a few hands on the tutorial software.

What follows is the training program I used before I sat down in the casino for the first time. I will also detail some of the ongoing methods that I am still using to improve my game. I realize that studying, practicing, and learning more in conjunction with live play is the only way to improve my game.

Chapter 49
Reading

I believe that reading is the fundamental key to learning anything new. Of course, merely reading about a subject will not teach you everything you need to know, but it will give you the basic foundation you need to build on. It has been said that a person who reads about a given subject for 30 minutes a day for a year will know more about that subject than 95 percent of the population. While there is no way to actually measure this number, I'm sure there is quite a bit of truth to it. Imagine sitting at the poker table and knowing more about the game than most of your opponents!

This is not as far-fetched as it may seem, especially at the low-limit level. There are many players sitting down to play every day who have never read one single book about Texas Hold'em. If they have read any books, it seems they must have skipped the chapter about selecting starting hands. And playing position.

It was only natural that the first step of my poker education would begin with reading. The first book I read was David Sklansky's *Hold'em Poker*. It was written in 1976 and updated in 1997. Sklansky is considered to be one of the foremost poker strategists. The ranking of starting hands he set forth has become a standard for most winning players. The hands listed in my arrow chart are based in part on his rankings although adjusted for low-limit games.

Sklansky's book started my poker education. My poker library quickly grew as I searched for more information to improve my game. Since that time, I have read numerous books about the game and some of them are listed in the reference section at the end of this book. I make it a point to read a little every day. Poker books are not like novels. I have re-read many of them as I gained experience. There are some situations that I did not fully understand until I came across them in a live game. Going back to the books allowed me to fully comprehend what happened during my playing session and gave me insight on how to handle the situation the next time I encountered it.

The first few months I spent at least an hour a day reading about Texas Hold'em. Books were not the only source of my reading material about the game. At the time, there were two good magazines published with articles by some of the top players and experts. Free copies of *Poker Digest* and *Card Player* were available at both the Mohegan Sun and Foxwoods Casinos where I did most of my early playing. *Poker Digest* is no longer published.

The Internet is another source of poker articles and information. The news group RGP, *rec.gambling.poker*, is an interactive forum of thousands of players whose skill level runs from professional to novice. The Two Plus Two Web site (*www.twoplustwo.com*) also has an excellent forum. You will find some unique strategies and ideas discussed there. If you have a question, you can post it to the group and receive many different answers. There are also many excellent Web sites devoted strictly to poker. Part of my duties as the Guide for the About Casino Gambling site is to search for the best sites offering relevant information about my topic. Searching for poker sites afforded me an opportunity to read a lot of information about Texas Hold'em online. You can find more poker links on my site at: *www.casinogambling.about.com*.

Reading is a vital part of learning but I'm not saying you should take everything you read at face value. Many times there will be conflicting opinions. This is especially true of some of the information you will read online. The more you read about a subject, the more views you will be exposed to. By reading a lot of different views about Hold'em, you will gain insight and be able to assimilate the information while weeding out the fiction from the facts. Some information works better in higher-limit games than in the games with lower limits.

When I wasn't reading about the game, I spent many hours just thinking about the information that I had read. I then put this information to practical use when I started playing hands of Texas Hold'em on my computer.

Chapter 50

Computer Software

After reading about the game the next step in my training program was to practice on the computer. I believe the best way to learn a casino game is to use tutorial software. I regularly recommend this approach to players who want to learn to play casino games. This allows players to learn the game before they risk real money in the casino. When I made the decision to learn how to casino poker I wanted to find a software program that would allow me to learn the basics of the game. *Turbo Texas Hold'em* by Wilson Software had all the features I was looking for and more.

When you begin the program you can modify the game settings to set up the game to match any rules or betting limits you will find in the casino. There are several other options to choose table display, how the cards are dealt during play and when new players will be introduced, along with sound and animation choices. I set the options to play a $3/$6 game and spent my first few hours with the program just getting a feel for how the game was played. The program has an automatic advisor that will assist you in making correct decisions. Before the flop, it will advise you as to which hands are playable for your position. You can chose the quick advise that advises you to check, call, raise, or fold or click on the more detailed advice screen that will show you:

Type of Hand: pair, connector, gapped
Your Position: early middle late
Pot Status: How many callers
Recommendation: check, call, raise, or fold

After the flop there are nine sets of strategies based on the number of opponents. The advisor may show multiple recommendations in many situations. As with before the flop, it will advise you of the proper decision to make.

There is a button that will allow you to access a screen to show you the odds at any time, either before or after the flop. This display screen shows you the pot odds and also your odds of making any particular hand based on the cards you are holding. As I became more familiar with the importance of odds, I started accessing this screen more to see the reasoning behind the advice given by the program.

One feature of the program that is helpful is the option to "zip" to the beginning of a new hand after you fold. If you are practicing your starting hands only and not working on reading the board, you don't have to wait until the whole hand is played out. This is a real time saver and will enable you to play hundreds of hands in a short amount of time.

After playing awhile you can evaluate your play. The program has a built-in analyzer that keeps track of all the hands played. When you click the "Stat" button you see statistical data for 12 different categories including play evaluation. Bar charts show if you have been playing too tight, too aggressive, too loose, or too passive.

Turbo Texas Hold'em has another feature called Challenge Mike. Mike is the name given to the virtual player who plays according to the correct strategy programmed by the computer. You chose to have Mike play 50, 100, or 200 hands. You then play the same hands and see if you can win more or lose less than Mike. This option is an excellent way to judge your play. If you lose $30 and Mike wins $70 then you have committed some severe errors. No matter how long my practice sessions last with the computer, I always end them by challenging Mike to 50 hands. I make it a practice to do this daily even if I have don't have time for a longer session.

If you want an even more detailed critique of your play, you can use Wilson's add on program called *Sidewinder Sid*. After any number of hands you can click on the Analysis button and Sid will pop up and review your play. The *Sidewinder Sid Analysis Program* provides a detailed hand by hand review of any errors you may have committed during your play. Sidewinder Sid is a cartoon character that uses Microsoft Text-to-Speech Technology to come to life. You can receive a detailed review of each hand. You can also get an over-all review of your play before the flop, after the flop, on the turn and on the river.

When you use *Sidewinder Sid* it is like having your own per-sonal coach. This detailed analysis has helped me immensely in learning to make the correct playing decisions. I use Sid in conjunc-tion with my daily Challenge Mike sessions. The program will also run high-speed simulations. Some of the results of these simulations appear elsewhere in this book.

Some players I talked to said they doubted that poker could be learned with a software program because in live poker you are play-ing against real people with unique personalities who play their hand differently. *Turbo Texas Hold'em* by Wilson Software showed me that this line of reasoning was outdated.

Wilson software solved this problem by programming profiles and traits in each of the virtual opponents you will face when play-ing. There are numerous sets of line-ups of players you can choose from to challenge. Some of these mirror aggressive, loose, low limit, moderate, or tight playing styles. You can even program your own opponents with the traits and playing style of anyone you might meet in the poker room. In a real game, players bet, call, raise, re-raise, and fold based on the value of their hands, the cards showing on the table, and their playing style. The computer players in Wilson's software act like real players and do this as well.

Although you won't be able to pick up physical tells, you will be able to ascertain certain patterns in playing style and starting hand selection. Many players are starting to play live poker at various Internet Web sites. When playing on these sites, you don't have the opportunity to see your opponents. If you are experienced in detect-ing patterns from your computer practice, it may actually be an advantage if you do decide to play online.

The other point that is often brought up about learning from computer software is the fact that a player is not risking real money and may get into a habit of playing too many hands. I think an intel-ligent player who is determined to improve his game will not have this problem. While practicing, I have experimented with playing bad hands and certain hands out of position to find out the conse-quences of my action. If anything, it reinforces the reasoning for not playing this way.

I played over 5,000 hands using the Wilson software before I ultimately sat down at a table in the casino. By that time I was confident that I was playing solid starting hands and making correct decisions based on the knowledge I had gained from my computer practice sessions. However, before that first live game I also did some additional training to make sure I was ready for the challenge.

Note: You can download a free demo version of Wilson's *Turbo Hold'em Software* by visiting their Web site at: *www.wilsonsoftware.com*.

Chapter 51

Flashcards

I attended elementary school back in the Stone Age around 15 BC. That is, **B**efore **C**alculators. All math problems were solved using longhand calculations with paper and pencil. To accomplish this it was required that we learn the multiplication and division tables by heart. We had to learn the tables by repetition, practicing them over and over until we had them memorized. To aid us in our learning efforts the teacher employed one of the oldest learning tools: the flashcard.

A flashcard was a big card (usually about 4"x6") with a problem on the front and the answer on the back. For example: "3x3" would be written on the front and the answer "9" would be printed on the back. One student would stand in front of the class and display the cards over and over as the class called out the answer in unison. Later a test was given and those failing found themselves in the corner with the flashcards for some solo practice or, worse, a one-on-one with the teacher after school.

Flashcards weren't fancy and seem pretty primitive by today's standards but they were effective in teaching rudimentary math skills and anything else that required memorizing information. I have used them in my adult life on many occasions.

When I learned to play blackjack the personal computer was barely affordable and all of the software programs were business related. To aid me in learning basic strategy, I resorted to the learning tool of my youth. I made flashcards with my starting hand front and the proper playing decision on the back based on the dealer's up card. I found that this was an excellent way to learn basic strategy.

The Arrow Chart of starting hands I designed was good as a quick reference to the position that certain hands could be played from but it did lack additional information as to how to play them. I then made the quick reference list that explains how to play the hands from each position. These are the lists shown after the section for each playing position. As I studied this list, I immediately thought of using flash cards to help me learn the proper play of each hand.

I took a sheet of pre-perforated business cards that I purchased from the office supply store and printed the starting hand on the front and the position and playing information on the back.

Having made the cards I could now shuffle them and glance through them at random. I would read the front of the card and note the position and playing criteria. If I were unsure of how to play a particular hand I would check the back of the card.

Now I realize that the playing of any poker hand is not set in stone as it is in blackjack. You do not want to play each hand automatically the same way every time. If you did a sharp opponent could easily read you and know how you would play in any given situation. I made these flashcards to give me a general guideline for playing each hand. I wanted to be able to quickly recognize the correct position for general circumstances only.

I found that the flashcards were extremely helpful for learning the Hold'em starting hands, just as they were in learning blackjack basic strategy. I carried them with me for about a week, running through the deck when I had a spare moment. The flashcards are easy to make and I recommend this approach for others who may be looking for a more effective way to remember the general guidelines for starting hands and the respective positions from which to play them.

Let me state again that the flashcards were used for learning the *general guidelines* for starting hands and I am not advocating playing each hand the same way in all circumstances.

Chapter 52
Videos

As part of my training program, I advise new players to watch a videotape about the game they want to learn. Watching videotapes can help teach you the mechanics of the game. You will actually see how the game is dealt and the bets are made so you will be familiar with the procedures and protocols when you sit down at a table. Videotapes can help reinforce what you have read and perhaps clear up any questions by visually showing you how the game is played. As they say, a picture is worth a thousand words.

There are not as many videos about poker as there are for other casino games. I did purchase two Texas Hold'em tapes to incorporate into my training session.

Texas Hold'em Poker (Fundamentals for Winning) by Fifth Street Video

This was the first tape I viewed and it is a good tape for beginners. It explained how the game is played. This included explaining the blinds, dealer button, and betting procedures. Although all of the mechanics of the game were covered, it showed the game being played in a home environment rather than in a cardroom. This tape also discussed in detail how to choose a starting hand and how to play it after the flop.

How to Beat Winning Hold'em Players by Ben Tracy and Joe Marks

This was the second tape I viewed and I found it more advanced than the first one. It states on the cover that it is not a tape for beginners or first-time Hold'em players. It does not spend a lot of time on the mechanics of the game but covers more of the strategy involved with playing winning Hold'em. The tape recommends playing with a tight-aggressive strategy and suggests limiting starting hands to develop the discipline needed to win. The tape also covers, in part, patterns of winning players; compares the skill vs. luck factors; and talks about the importance of money management and discipline.

Both of these tapes stressed the importance of playing quality starting hands and solid play after the flop, but neither showed the game being played in a casino cardroom. Even though I felt that I had a good understanding of the mechanics, I decided to take a ride down to the casino and actually watch a live game being played.

Chapter 53
Railbirding

In some casinos, the area for the poker tables is separated from the main casino floor by a railing or some other physical barrier. This keeps the spectators out of the way of the players but allows them to watch the action. Because spectators line up along the rail to watch, they are sometimes referred to as "railbirds."

I wanted to watch a few games to get an idea of the table procedures and protocols so I decided to take a ride to the casino and become a railbird for a few hours. I visited Foxwoods Casino in Connecticut. Foxwoods is the world's largest casino and has a first-class poker room. Many casinos now have the poker tables in a separate room. There is enough space to allow spectators to walk around the tables instead of being limited to watching from a rail.

I looked at the sign-in board at the registration desk and found out which tables were hosting the low-limit Texas Hold'em games. I walked over to a spot where I could observe the action at one of the tables while being out of the way. I stood about mid table so I could get a clear view of the board.

In the beginning, I worked on reading the board as the dealer turned over the cards. After a few hands, I started concentrating on the players. I wanted to observe the types of hands they were playing. I noticed that many of them seemed to be playing any two cards without any regard to position. I saw players turning over hands that I would not have played from any position.

I observed one player who had the largest stack of chips. I watched this game for over an hour and saw him play only two hands, which he won. When he was involved in the hand he was raising after the flop in both instances. It was easy to detect that his was a tight-aggressive player.

As I was observing the game, I came to the conclusion that I could learn a lot about the players from watching as a spectator. If I were getting ready to sit down in this game I would have a wealth of information about the players seated at this table. In the future, I would recall this observation and it convinced me to start a procedure that I use whenever I play in a cardroom.

When you enter the poker room and sign in at the registration desk, you can't always get immediate seating at a table. You are put on a waiting list and your name is called when a seat opens up at the game you requested. Many players go grab a coffee, sit down and read, or just socialize with the other players waiting for a game. When I get put on the waiting list, I make it a habit of finding which tables are dealing the game I am waiting for. Often there is only one game going for the limit I want to play, so it is easy to find the table. I then find a place to stand where I can observe the game.

I start to make mental notes about the players at the table. I note what type of hands they are playing along with the number of pots they are active in. I notice who is doing the raising and try to find out what types of hands they are raising with. When I sit down in the game I know more about all the players than they know about me and, as they say, knowledge is power.

Had I not decided to do a little railbirding on that day, I may not have come to this conclusion so quickly. After watching the games, I continued my tour of the poker room. As I was walking around, I noticed a sign saying that they offered free poker lessons. I thought taking a lesson would be a perfect opportunity to get a little hands-on experience.

Chapter 54

Free Lessons

I always recommend that anyone who wants to learn a new casino game take advantage of the free lessons offered by the casinos. During the lesson, you are given a brief description of the game and the procedures involved in playing. Sitting in on a lesson gives you a chance to play the game using non-value chips. The instructor will point out if you make a mistake and advise you how to play correctly. Players can gain confidence before ever sitting down in a real game. When I saw that Foxwoods offered lessons for Texas Hold'em, I thought sitting down for a lesson would be a perfect opportunity for me to become acquainted with playing in a casino poker room. This way I wouldn't feel uncomfortable when the time came to join a live game.

It was a Saturday afternoon and I sat down at the training table joining five other people who were interested in learning to play Texas Hold'em. Our instructor was a fellow named Jerry who is a regular dealer in the poker room. We all introduced ourselves and the lesson got underway. Like myself, all of the other students had played some kitchen-table poker but none of us had every played Hold'em. Having been studying the game and playing on my computer, I felt light years ahead of the others, but I refrained from any comments as I sat there listening to the lesson.

Jerry handed out a stack of non-denomination chips to everyone and proceeded to explain how the game is played. He explained the reasons why Texas Hold'em was different from seven-card stud, which most of the others had played before.

He then went on to tell us a little about the betting procedures of the game, explaining about the blind bets to begin each hand. He told us that all casino poker is played for table stakes. This means the money you buy in with and have on the table is the money you play with. You are not allowed to reach into your pocket in the middle of a hand for more money. If the bet is more money than what you have on the table you can go "all in" which means that you will be playing for the pot your money is in. The rest of the players can continue betting. This money is put in a side pot and will be given to the player with the winning hand of those involved in the side pot. Players may purchase additional chips between hands.

After his explanation of the game, he discussed a little strategy, advising us to play only strong starting hands especially from the early positions. He told us that he sees too many players who sit down at the table and expect to bet every hand they are given. He said these are the players that go broke very quickly.

Now it was time to play a few hands to get the feel of the game. One person was selected as the dealer and the players to the left of the dealer button posted the small and big blinds. Jerry explained that a new player sitting down to a game that is in progress has to either post a bet equal to the big blind or wait until the big blind gets around to his position before entering the game. He also explained that the big blind is a live bet. If other players call without raising, the big blind has the option to check or raise. Too often a new player will inadvertently throw his hand in without realizing that he has already bet that round. We played a few rounds until everyone felt comfortable with the procedures involved in playing the game.

Not all casinos offer poker lessons. If you are planning on visiting a casino, you can call ahead to the poker room and see if they have lessons available. The Excalibur Casino in Las Vegas is another casino that has offered lessons to players over the years. If the casino you visit doesn't offer lessons, you can get a feel for the game by watching from the rail and observing the players.

After the lesson was over, Jerry suggested that we might want to practice by playing in the low-limit tournament that is held weekly on Saturday mornings. I joked that it was probably filled with sharks waiting to devour unsuspecting players that dare venture into their territory. He laughed and said it was a low-limit tournament that attracted players of all skill levels. He said because of the low entry fee many of the players were beginners or average players just out to have a good time without risking a lot of money in a live game. After investigating this, I thought it would be the perfect opportunity for me to gain some practical playing experience and get the feel of a live game.

Chapter 55

Low-Limit Tournaments

Before I started learning about casino poker, whenever I heard the words "Poker Tournament," I immediately thought of the World Series of Poker. The WSOP final event has a $10,000 entry fee. I was under the impression that all poker tournaments were played only for high stakes by professional players. I was wrong about that. There are tournaments held all over the country that are designed to attract players by offering a variety of entry fees. Whether it is low limit or high stakes you're looking for, you can probably find a tournament near you.

Foxwoods holds different tournaments six days a week. The Saturday morning event is a Limit Hold'em tournament. The cost of the tournament is $20. This consists of a $15 buy-in and a $5 entry fee. Players receive $1,000 in tournament chips. There is also one optional re-buy if you go broke, or you can just add it onto your existing chips. The $10 re-buy will get you another $1,000 in tournament chips. The re-buy must be made during the first two rounds of play. Most players looking to make it to the finals take advantage of this option. The prize pool contains 100 percent of all money from the buy-ins and re-buys. As an added bonus Foxwoods credits your player's club account with $10 in comp, which can be used for merchandise, shows, or food.

Tournament structures can vary in the amount of the buy-ins, number of levels played, and the amount of time to play each level. All tournaments have one thing in common. You are trying to win all the chips from all the other players. The money from the prize pool is divided up among the players reaching the final table. The lion's share goes to the winner, while the runners-up receive a lesser percentage. You have a limited number of chips determined by the buy-in and re-buy. When you lose all your chips, you are out of the tournament.

The structure of the Foxwoods tournament is as follows: There are 14 levels with each level being played for 20 minutes. The blinds increase after each level of play. There are ten players to each starting table. There may be 11 or nine at a table if there is an odd number of entrants. The prize money is based on the number of players entered in the tournament.

I decided that entering the tournament would be a great learning experience for me. I am aware that in tournament play the strategy becomes a little more challenging at the higher levels, but I was looking to gain experience and practice the discipline needed to play solid starting hands. It would give me a chance to learn table etiquette and gain confidence in my playing abilities while interacting with other players.

It had been a month since I had picked up my educational material. Since that time I had been reading the books, watching the videotapes, and playing thousands of hands using Wilson's Turbo Hold'em Software. I was ready. The lyrics of a popular song started echoing in my head: "Put me in coach, I'm ready to play the game!"

The week after my free poker lesson, I decided to take the plunge and enter the low-limit Texas Hold'em tournament at Foxwoods. I could tell you that I was cool and calm as I entered the poker room, but that would be a lie. My adrenaline level was on the upper end of the spectrum. Somehow the casino had taken on a new air of excitement and wonder. I was about to enter unknown territory. I had a feeling of anticipation as if I were climbing the first peak of the Desperado roller coaster at Buffalo Bills Casino, anticipating with a certain nervous energy the 200 ft. plunge that would that send me on an 80-mile-an-hour thrill ride. I admit that lately I had become somewhat complacent in the casino and I hadn't felt this excited since the first time I bellied up to the craps table years ago when I decided to learn that game.

I approached the tournament registration counter and gave them my player's card and $20 fee. I was handed my entry slip with "table 9, seat 6" printed on it. I was told to keep the slip handy because they would need to sign it if I decided to use my one time re-buy. I proceeded to the table and took my seat. It was 9:50 A.M. The tournament started at 10. The table quickly filled up. As we sat down, the dealer checked our slips and handed us $1,000 in tournament chips. Each level of play is 20 minutes long. There is a ten-minute break after the fourth level. My goal was to make it to the first break. At 10 A.M. the tournament director announced there were 112 players and they would be paying 18 places. He then proceeded to tell the dealers to "Shuffle up and deal!"

The button started at the number ten spot on the table. That meant I would be in the middle position for the first hand. Before I sat down, I told myself that I would play a tight game by playing only the early position hands for the starting few rounds. My main objective was to get the feel of the game and learn the protocols and procedure so I would feel comfortable in the weeks to come when I was ready to sit in a live game.

The very first hand I was dealt was the 8 of clubs and 3 of diamonds. Not quite the worst hand of 2 and 7 off suit, but pretty close. I folded. A few hands later I was in the big blind with a J-7. There were three callers and I checked the option. The flop brought no help and I folded after there was a bet. That was the only hand I played at level one. I took my re-buy before round two, giving me an additional $1,000 in chips.

One humorous incident occurred in level two. One player in early position raised immediately. The flop brought Q-Q-9. He bet and had four callers. The turn was another 9, making two pair on the board. He bet and all the players called him. The river was a King. He bet and again they all called him. He turned over a pair of deuces and announced that he had "Three Pair." He was upset when the dealer explained that only five cards play. A player with a full house ultimately won the hand but everyone had a good chuckle.

My first win came near the end of level-two play. I was dealt a pair of Kings and I raised. The player to my left (Player 2) called and the player to his left (Player 3) re-raised. Another player (Player 5) cold-called both raises. There is a maximum of three raises so I capped it. All of the players called. The flop brought a K-9-7. Three Kings for me. I bet and Player 2 folded. Player 3 raised and Player 5 called. I didn't feel the flop was a threat and didn't want to scare either of them off, so I called. The turn was a Jack. I bet and Player 3 called and Player 5 raised. I figured he had three Jacks and I re-raised him. Both called me. The River was a 6. I bet and both called me. I turned my three Kings. Player 3 had A-K in the hole for a pair of Kings with an Ace kicker. Player 5 turned over his pair of Jacks, my guess was correct. At this point I felt a rush. I scooped a big pot and it felt great. By the time the break came I had one other small win. I had only participated in about nine hands including the times I was in the blinds.

Good tight play had gotten me to the first break. By this time I had settled down and was comfortable with the procedures and protocol of the game. Any nervousness or apprehension had long given way to the pure excitement of the competition. I had $1,900 in chips to start level five. I also noticed that there were only six tables left out of the 11 that started the tournament. I had made it past many of the other players. Unfortunately, I didn't make it much farther that day. As the blinds increased, the quality of my hands decreased. After I was knocked out I made the following observations:

The tournament was a great learning experience.
You don't have to be an expert to compete.
Most players are friendly.
I have the confidence to be a competitive player.
It was a lot of fun!

The "tournament bug" had bitten me and I planned to enter more of these in the months ahead. I set a personal goal to make it to the final table before year's end. My next step was to play in my first live game.

Chapter 56

My First Game

After entering the low-limit tournament it was time to put it all together. I was ready to play my first live game in the cardroom.

I chose to play my first session at the Mohegan Sun in Connecticut. It is a little smaller and more intimate than the larger Foxwoods where I had played in the tournament. I had previously done a little railbirding there and liked the cardroom.

The Mohegan Sun has a sign up desk. When you enter the poker room you must sign in and tell the host what game you are interested in playing. If there is an immediate opening, you will be seated immediately. If the table is full, they will take your initials and call you when there is an opening. They don't have a board for the names. I chose the $3/$6 Hold'em game and was told there was an opening. Before sitting down I purchased my chips at the counter to take to the table with me.

The minimum buy-in for the $3/$6 game is $30.This is not very many chips if the betting gets aggressive. The last thing I wanted to do was be short of chips when I had a good hand. I chose to buy-in for $100 which is about 15 times the largest bet.

At the Mohegan Sun, when you first sit down at the table, you must post a bet equal to the big blind if you wish to play immediately. If not, you wait until it is your turn to be the big blind and enter the game then. I chose not to enter right away. By waiting it gave me a few hands to watch the other players and see how they were playing. Had I not gotten a seat right away, I would have watched the action from the rail while I was on the waiting list.

Once in the game, I was cautious to observe proper table etiquette and was careful not to make any of the common beginner mistakes that would give me away as a novice. I had decided on my game plan before I ever sat down at the table. I would play a tight game using mostly the early position starting hands that could be played from any position. I chose to limit my first session to an hour and a half to make sure I practiced discipline and maintained my concentration.

As I sat down at the table and waited for my turn to be the big blind I watched the other players. After participating in the tournament I felt comfortable enough with the table protocol and was not intimidated by the other players. The first 20 minutes at the table all I did was fold hand after hand. In between I just kept my eyes open and my mouth shut. Finally, I was rewarded with a suited Ace-Queen. I bet and was called by three other players. The flop was A-7-4 and I bet and was called again. The turn brought a King and I had one player call me all the way to the river. He turned his cards showing a King in the hole giving me my first win with a pair of Aces. I have to admit to a little adrenaline rush as I scooped my first pot. I was feeling pretty good but, a few hands later, my over-exuberance cost me some money as I chased everyone out of a pot early.

I had K-Q suited and the flop was K-Q-Q. I was second to act with a full house and instead of slow playing by calling the bet that was made before me, I raised immediately. This caused everyone, except the original bettor, to fold. He checked on the turn and then folded when I bet. If I had not been so impatient, and just called, I probably could have kept a couple players in the hand and collected a little more on the end.

I played a tight game and won a couple more pots during the game. I was ahead when I made my second and more costly mistake. I was the big blind with J-8. There were five callers. The flop was J-8-7 all different suits. This is known as a "rainbow." I had two pair and bet. I was called around and the turn brought a 9. I bet and all the players folded except one who raised me. I was only looking at my two pair and called the raise without hesitation. The river was a 3 and I checked. He bet and I called again. I was not paying as much attention to the board as I should have. He turned over his Q-T suited giving him a straight and leaving me wondering why I did not notice the straight possibility especially when I was raised on the turn. It was my mistake and put a little dent in my stack of chips.

After a few more hands my hour and a half was up. I collected my chips and headed for the cage. I cashed out with a $10 profit. I was a winner in my first game. I also learned a couple lessons that would stick with me.

What I discovered during my first game was that most of the players in a low-limit game are just average people. In fact, after watching some of the starting hands that were played, I would guess that a couple of them had never read a book or magazine article about Hold'em. I honestly felt that the training I had done up to this first match had proven to be a great asset for me. It was time well spent as I now felt comfortable with my play, and knew I had the ability to be competitive. I also knew that I had much more to learn but this would come in time. This first game showed me that if you can apply the discipline to wait for the proper starting hands, you will have a solid foundation to help you succeed at this game.

As I drove home from the casino I spent some time reflecting on the game and evaluating my play. I was looking forward to my next session. I was also looking forward to my next low-limit tournament.

Chapter 57
Tournament Strategy

After playing in my first tournament, I knew I could be competitive. I decided to play in more of these. I felt that my play was solid; I had made it past the first break, and further than many of the other players who had entered the tournament. I picked up a book about tournament play and began searching for information about winning low-limit tournaments.

During my first tournament I played very tight. I was just trying to get the feel for the game and thought my best chance for lasting was to play only the best hands. After doing some reading, I discovered that I had inadvertently stumbled upon the correct strategy for playing the early rounds of a tournament.

In low-limit tournaments, there are many players who are out to have a good time for a fixed minimum expense. In the opening rounds of the tournament, many of these players will play with the any two-card mentality because the betting limits are low and they have a lot of chips. You will also find many of the maniacs who will raise with any hand hoping to get lucky in the early rounds. As the betting levels escalate, they continue to play in this fashion and soon find themselves out of chips.

The proper strategy for these early rounds is to play tight while everyone else is playing very loose. By limiting myself to the premium starting hands, I was doing just that. It is what enabled me to make it through to the higher rounds. Since I was not playing many hands, it also gave me time to study the other players at the table. I was able to determine who was playing solid hands and who was not. This information would help in the later rounds.

During my second and third tournaments, I was able to make it past the second break, but not much further. I went back and did some more reading and I tried to analyze my game to determine what I was doing wrong. I discovered two problems. I was continuing to play too tight during the later rounds. I was also not playing as aggressively as I should have. I was limping in with hands that I should have been raising with. As the limits get higher in the middle rounds, players become very tight. A raise will narrow the field or even win outright, as players become more cautious.

I made some adjustments to my play and, during the fifth tournament that I played, I made it to my first final table. I finished ninth but was "in the money." I was paid $45 for ninth place less my $30 entry fee giving me a profit of $15 for the match.

The money, however, did not really matter to me. I am a competitive person by nature and the feeling of accomplishment that I experienced meant more to me than any money involved. I felt that I was making a significant improvement in my game. This was confirmed a month later when I accomplished the goal I had set after the first match.

I have adopted the following strategy for the early rounds of the tournament. It is tight and aggressive and has worked in getting me into the later rounds after many of the other players have busted out. Here are the hands I play in raised and unraised situations. (s) denotes suited cards.

Early Position

Raise and reraise with: **A-A, K-K, A-Ks**
Play: **Q-Q, A-Qs, K-Qs, A-K**
Raise with these hands or call one raise in a raised pot.

Middle Position

J-J, T-T, 9-9, 8-8, A-Js, A-Ts, K-Js, Q-Js, A-Q, K-Q
Raise if the hand has not been raised. Fold if pot was raised.

Late Position

Call: **A-Xs, K-Ts, Q-Ts, A-J, A-T, K-J, Any Pair, and Suited connectors**—with four or more players.
If raised, fold.

During the later rounds of the tournament you will need to shift gears and loosen up a little. Space does not permit going into the complete tournament strategy. There are several good tournament books for those wishing to learn more. Using this strategy for the early rounds will get you started on your way to solid tournament play.

Chapter 58

Tournament Win

I entered the tournament on Saturday June 17, 2000. There were 78 players with 74 re-buys. The total tournament chips in play, $152,000.

I started the tournament and won a small hand in level one. When we started level two, I made a re-buy giving me another $1,000 in chips. I had awful luck. I raised with pocket Jacks only to get beaten by Kings. The next hand I had pocket 7s and lost that one. I also raised with pocket Queens and had those beaten. At the end of level two, I had only $700 left. I thought I would be lucky to make it to the first break.

I did nothing in level three, but came back with a big hand before the break. I had $2,175 in chips at the break. I was moved to two different tables after the first break, I held my own in levels 5 and 6 and 7. My last move was to table one where I had $8,000 right before the second break. At the second break there were 12 players left. Nine would make it to the final table. The blinds were $1,000 and $1,500. I stole the small blind. Two players were knocked out the next hand and the final table was set. We drew numbers for seats. I drew the five seat. I had $9,000 starting the final table. I was number seven out of nine for chip position. The chip leader was a woman who had stacks of $1,000 chips. I honestly thought she had a lock on the number one spot. I remember thinking I would play tight and hope the two players with fewer chips would get out before me. A funny thing happened.

One of the players with fewer chips was named Phil. He had $3,000 and drew the number one seat making him the small blind. He had to post $1,500. He folded the first hand and I did the same. The next hand I looked at my cards and found Pocket Rockets staring at me. I thought to myself, this is it. I'm either going out with a blaze of glory, or taking it to the bank. The player under the gun called all in and I raised. Everyone folded to Phil who went all in. The small blind called and John the big blind re-raised me. I capped it all in. The flop was Ah-7c-8c. The Turn was Jack of hearts. The river brought a Ten of hearts. John turned over pocket Kings. I had three Aces to take the side pot. Phil turned K-Q of hearts for a Royal Flush. He won the smaller original pot and got a free Foxwoods jacket for having a Royal Flush. I was lucky that Phil was all in otherwise I would have been eliminated. This was the turning point of the game for me.

I got a few powerful hands in a row. I played them aggressively and started hitting the flops. As the blinds went up the players all became more cautious. I was accumulating chips and started to get more aggressive. As I did I was winning more hands. I was in the zone, because all of a sudden I remember someone saying, "Looks like a new chip leader. I looked down at my stack of $1,000 chips and realized it was I. One player made another comment about me grabbing all the chips. I smiled and said I must be a "Chip Magnet." That moniker stuck with me the rest of the match. Being the chip leader wields a certain amount of power. I was able to take a lot of hands by bullying my way with raises. I did use a certain tactic. I made sure that I would occasionally show my big winning hand after everyone folded. This way they were never sure if I was bluffing or had the power to back up the bets. Now I was able to coast a little and let a few other players knock each other out. When we started the final round I was hoping to be able to outlast a few of the players to gain more of the prize money. By the time we got down to four, I had only one thing on my mind: winning! At this point I did not care about the prize money I did not want any deals cut. I wanted to be able to walk away with the win.

We were finally down to three players. I had six or seven times more chips as the woman who was the original chip leader when we started the final table. Dale, the number three player, was a little behind her and asked her if she wanted to chop the money for second and third. She said no way. She eventually lost to him. Now there were the two of us. Dale asked me if I wanted to make a deal—I said, "No thank you." I had him by a substantial lead and I had to see this through. We battled back and forth but the cards were holding out for me. The blinds were $5,000 and $10,000.

On the final hand I posted the small blind and Dale posted the $10,000 big blind, leaving him with $4,000. I was dealt pocket 8s. I called and he raised all in, and the dealer dealt the final cards. 4-4-2-T.

He flipped over an Ace and 6 and said, "You better be able to beat this." I turned over my pocket 8s. I extended my hand and said, "Nice match." He shook it and congratulated me on my win. It's hard to describe my feelings at the end. The adrenaline rush and excitement of my first tournament win will stay with me for a long time. It is definitely one of the most memorable experiences I have had in the casinos.

I have the utmost respect for all the players who competed in the tournament. I did not see one incident of poor sportsmanship. I also have a great deal of respect for the staff and dealers at Foxwoods. They run a first-class tournament.

I took the next week off to fly to Las Vegas for vacation. I returned two weeks later and repeated my first-place finish. Two first place finishes in a row added to my desire to play more tournaments. Since then, I have made many more final table appearances, and have had many more tournament wins.

Chapter 59

Friends and Networking

It is always easier to learn something new if you have someone you can ask for advice or someone to share ideas with. I sought out my friend and co-worker Jack when I made the decision to learn how to play casino poker. Jack is an excellent Seven-Card Stud player, who has over six years experience playing winning poker. I asked him some questions about playing in the casino and poker in general. I told him I had decided to learn how to play Texas Hold'em. He said that he had just started learning the game himself. He wanted to expand his horizons and have another game to play when the waiting list for stud got too long. The timing was perfect, as now we both would have someone to discuss the game and strategies with.

I attribute part of my early success with the game to the discussions that we had. I learned that some of the situations I encountered at the table were not unique, as Jack had similar experiences as he was learning the game. This is one of the advantages to having someone you can talk with honestly about the game.

In the poker room you will meet many different people. If possible you should try to strike up a friendship with other players. Since you already have something in common, it will probably not be too difficult. Some will only be looking out for themselves and will be trying to get an angle on any player they may eventually be playing against. However, many of them are nice people who you will become friendly with if you become a regular at your local cardroom. If you can cultivate a friendship with someone you trust and can share ideas with you, you will both benefit. Some friendships will develop under strange circumstances.

During my first tournament win at Foxwoods, the match was down to me and three other players. The gentleman I knocked out in fourth position before winning the match was a player named John. He was a true gentleman and was the first to congratulate me after the match was over. We began talking and I explained that I had been learning to play the game and writing about my experiences for my About.com Web site over the last few months. I gave him my card and he e-mailed me the next day to compliment me on my poker articles.

We met at the tournament the next week and, after it was over, John and his son, Dan, and I held an extensive conversation about Texas Hold'em. It was easy to tell that we were both serious about improving our games. We started sharing strategies and had discussions about the game via e-mail. A few months later at the WPO held at Foxwoods, John introduced me to a few of his friends, one of whom is a professional poker player.

Over the next year I met several more players as John had started a little e-mail group. We participate almost daily in discussions about the game through e-mails and ICQ chat. We all became close friends even though some of us did not meet face to face until months after our group had formed. None of us were hesitant about sharing our strategies with each other and we all benefited from our combined knowledge.

Networking is a word that is sometimes used for developing professional contacts that can be beneficial to all parties involved. When you try to establish friendships in the cardroom, you are in essence "networking." In the poker world, the biggest network of players is the Rec. Gambling Poker Newsgroup on the Internet. Thousands of players share ideas daily via e-mail and network amongst themselves. In a way, our little group could be considered a smaller private network of dedicated poker players. That's the way it started but it soon became a group of trusted friends who have all helped each other to improve.

It just goes to show you how friendships can develop under strange circumstances. John was a gracious loser and our conversation when he congratulated me after the tournament turned into a winning situation for both of us. Don't hesitate to talk with other players or congratulate a winner. You may just make a friend or two who can help you improve your game.

Chapter 60
Online Practice

Free Online Play

A philosopher once said, "nothing ventured—nothing gained." In business we often hear that there are no rewards without risk. Athletic trainers say, "No pain, no gain!"

The statements above are often echoed when the subject of playing online live poker for free cyber chips is discussed. There is an ongoing debate about whether practicing at many of the free Internet poker sites has any value to a player learning the game.

The biggest complaint about the free Internet games is that the players are not risking any money. The free play poker sites give each player a certain amount of money to play with. Some sites will replenish a player's bankroll as soon as he goes broke, while others will make him wait a day before being granted more money. Either way, since a player has no fear of ever going broke, he will often play with an "any two-card" mentality for starting hands. Once in a hand they will play "No Fold'em Hold'em" and call each hand to the river.

I agree that many of the players in the free games are bad players, and it can lead to the deterioration of your game if you start emulating the other bad players. Players have a tendency to lower their standards when they are playing for fun. If a new player sees this going on, he may adopt a similar playing style, which will be fatal once he sits down in a live game. However, I do believe that there is something to be gained from practicing online.

Mechanics

If you are new to Texas Hold'em you can learn the mechanics of the game while playing online. Watching and participating in a game will make you comfortable with the procedures and protocol of the game.

Discipline

Discipline is one of the most important traits you will need to be a winning player. You can practice discipline by adopting a real game approach to your online session.

Reading the Board

Learning to read the board is another skill that can be practiced when you play online. You will have plenty of opportunity to do this, as the play online is much faster than it is in a live game.

Paying Attention

You should be watching the other players' starting hands at the showdown to see what hands they are playing. This is something you should be doing in live games. Get in the habit of doing it every time you play online. It will help you develop your attention to the game. You should be able to determine who is playing tight or loose by the hands they are showing at the end.

Practicing online can be like any other endeavor. You get out of it what you put into it. If you treat these free games as if you were playing with real money, then you can learn from them. If you decided to just play any two cards to the river, you are defeating the purpose. You are also wasting your time and running the risk of developing bad habits.

Small-Stakes Online Play

After some free practice you may want to try playing for very small stakes online before heading to the cardroom for the first time. There are a number of reputable online sites that are now catering to millions of players every day. In the first printing of this book I suggested that you limit online play to practice in the free games. I still suggest that all new players get some free practice before putting their money at risk in a live game; however, my views about online poker have changed. I am now convinced that it is safe, secure, and a great alternative for many players who are not able to make a trip to a cardroom without traveling long miles to play poker for a few hours. There are actually several other advantages to playing online.

Lower Stakes

Online you can play for very low stakes. Since there are no dealers, rental fees, or utilities to pay, the online sites can offer games at very low limits that would not be practical or profitable in a brick-and-mortar cardroom. If you are a new player, you can find some sites with stakes as low as a nickel or a dime. It is a great way to make the transition from free play to money play.

No Intimidation

Sitting down in a live game and facing nine other players can be very intimidating for a new player. Playing online poker is akin to playing a video game, as you are sitting in front of your computer facing a monitor instead of a live person. You can interact with the other players via the chat box or choose to just play your own game without having to talk or socialize. Nobody can see you, and if your hands are shaking because of nerves nobody can see that, either.

Fits Your Schedule

Online play fits your schedule, because you can play anytime you want 24/7. No traveling time is involved and there is little or no waiting to get into a game once you are logged on.

Everybody Acts in Turn

Because of the software used in online games, nobody can act out of turn. Some sites have buttons or boxes you can check so you can choose to fold, call, or raise as soon as you see your cards, but these actions will not take place until it is your turn to act.

Keep Notes

In a live game you may not know another player's name, but online each player's screen name is in plain view. It is easy to keep accurate notes about the other players you meet online—the types of hands they play, or whether they're passive, aggressive, tight, or loose. Nobody can see you writing, so you can be as detailed as you want to be.

Safety Concerns

One of my biggest concerns about online poker was the idea of collusion among players. Online players have numerous ways to communicate with each other—for instance, via ICQ instant messenger, or even over the telephone. But collusion happens in brick-and-mortar cardrooms as well, and in a cardroom it is not often easy to spot. Once the dealer mucks the cards the hand is over and it is hard to prove anything improper went on. This is not the case, however, when you are playing online.

The operators of online sites have a recorded history of all hands that have been played by each and every player. Many of the sites use special software programs to track the betting patterns of players suspected of collusion. They can review every hand played by the parties involved and look for anything out of the ordinary.

With new technology and vast improvements in encryption and security, the chance of someone hacking your game is not really an issue. Nobody can see your cards as you play except you. Online poker sites use the same technology that is used by online banks and other financial sites. If you are not worried about banking or trading stocks online, you shouldn't be concerned playing low-limit poker either.

If you want to try online poker I would suggest you pick a site that offers free games as well as money games. Download their software and play free games for a while to make sure you like the way the software plays and the graphics look.

Chapter 61

Moving Ahead

I have often heard the expression, "A little knowledge can be dangerous."

There can be some truth to that statement if the person who gains the knowledge stops learning after attaining only a small amount of information about a subject. Anyone who thinks he knows it all is only kidding himself and setting himself up for possible disaster.

I once had a manager who berated employees for trying anything new. He would yell and holler as he told all of us that he had been doing the job the same way for 30 years and would continue to do so. We should either do things his way or seek employment elsewhere. It didn't matter that technology was changing the industry around him, making his methods quite antiquated. Fortunately upper management finally stepped in and removed him and his stagnant philosophy.

Some poker players have a similar outlook about the game as my former manager had about his job. They learn to play the game using a certain style and then proceed to play the same way, day in and day out, never advancing beyond the basics and refusing to learn anything new. I have no intention of letting that happen to me.

I will forever be a student of the game. I am constantly looking for ways to improve my game. The day I think I know it all will be the day that I will quit playing. Since I started playing the game, I have not played a single session where I have not learned something new. Some of my new knowledge comes from mistakes that I make while playing and some of it comes from observing other players at the table. At the end of each session, I critique my play to see what I did wrong or could have done better. I am constantly on the lookout for new books, articles, or other material to read about the game. The methods I described in the training section are methods that I still use in my ongoing education.

I have had the opportunity to meet and talk to many winning players including some who play professionally. All of them agree that the secret to becoming a better player is really no secret at all. It's a matter of continually studying the game, learning from mistakes, practicing strategies, and keeping an open mind to new ideas.

Rather than the statement above about knowledge being dangerous, I prefer the statement, "A little knowledge is an excellent start!"

Here is a little knowledge that you can use to start improving your game immediately as you move forward with your poker education. Here are seven tips that you can incorporate into your game with very little effort.

The Magnificent Seven

1. Be more selective
Stop playing with the any two-card can win attitude. Once you tighten the standards for your starting hands your game should improve. This also means playing the hands you choose to play in correct position.

2. Don't automatically call the small blind.
Players lose more money by automatically calling from the small blind with a hand that has very little chance of winning. You will be in the small blind about three times per hour. In a $3/$6 game, it will cost you $2 to complete the bet from the small blind. The average win rate for this limit game is $6 per hour or the same amount it is costing you to complete your bet from the small blind.

3. Stop playing any Ace.

Stop playing a single Ace. Most of the other players will be doing the same and it will cost you money when you pair your Ace with a weak kicker.

4. Don't cold-call with weak hands.

Stop cold calling raises before the flop unless your have a very powerful hand such as A-A, K-K, or A-K. Raises from early position usually mean a strong hand.

5. Don't draw to the idiot end.

Don't draw to the low end of a straight. The majority of the time you will be beaten by a higher straight.

6. Overcards on the Turn.

In a multiway pot, you should not be calling on the Turn with just overcards if that is your only out. If there is a bet, it usually means someone has at least a pair. If there is a raise, you know you should fold without hesitation.

7. Pair on board

When a pair flops you should abandon your straight and flush draws. The odds of your opponent making a full house are about the same as your straight or flush draw.

If you follow these seven little tips, you should notice a big improvement in your results at the table.

Chapter 62

Closing Thoughts

I hope you have learned something from this book. If you are new to the game, I encourage you to try some of the methods I used to learn how to play Texas Hold'em. I can't guarantee that you will have the same success as I had, but I can attest that these methods worked for me. Hopefully this book will help you make the transition from the kitchen to the cardroom. If you already play the game, I hope you have learned some new ways to improve your game.

I started my project to learn about casino poker so I could share the information with the readers on my Web site. I wanted to prove that it was possible for a player with no previous knowledge of Texas Hold'em, to learn how to play winning poker in a relatively short period of time. In the process, I discovered a game that I truly enjoy playing and one that I profit from as well. Texas Hold'em is one of the most exciting games I have ever played.

For me, playing Texas Hold'em is not just about money. I am a competitive person by nature. I enjoy the heat of the battle, as I match wits against the other players. It is one of the reasons I also enjoy playing in the low-limit tournaments.

In all honesty, you will never get rich playing in low-limit games. Therefore you must enjoy the game. If you are a winning player, you will get more enjoyment out of the game. I hope this book has given you the foundation you will need to help you win.

My recommendations for starting hands may be a little tighter than those recommended by some others. I advocate playing a tighter game while you are learning, to allow you to concentrate on the other aspects of the game. Once you start playing winning Texas Hold'em, and gain more experience, you will be able to adjust your game to fit your style.

I urge you to continue reading and learning more about the game. I recommend the following books if you would like to further your Texas Hold'em education. As I always say:

"Luck comes and goes . . . knowledge stays forever!"

Winning Low-Limit Hold'em **by Lee Jones**

This book is written specifically for low-limit players. It does not cover a lot of advanced poker theory, but rather focuses on solid poker play that will help you win in low-limit games. Whether you are a beginner or experienced low-limit player, you will learn some valuable information from this book. Lee Jones writes for a national poker magazine and has an extensive knowledge of the game.

Hold'em Excellence **and** *More Hold'em Excellence* **by Lou Krieger**

Both books by Lou Krieger will help you improve your Texas Hold'em game. Lou has a unique way of explaining the concepts needed to win at Texas Hold'em that is easily understood by the novice as well as the advanced player.

Hold'em Poker **by David Sklansky**

This book was one of the first books written about Texas Hold'em. It was originally written in 1976 and was updated in 1997. Sklansky introduced the concepts of slow playing and semi-bluffing. The chart of starting hands has become the standard for winning players.

Hold'em's Odds Book **by Mike Petriv**

This book will teach you how to do the mathematics to figure the odds in the game of Texas Hold'em. You will need an understanding of basic math to follow all the examples. Even if you don't learn to do the calculations on your own, the charts supplied in the book contain valuable information for every player.

Card Player Magazine

This magazine is an excellent source of information to help you improve your game. You will find articles from some of the top poker players in the world. Most cardrooms have complimentary issues of this bi-weekly magazine.

Glossary

Action: Any betting, calling, raising, or other act made by a player can be referred to as action. If a player calls your bet, you are getting action.

Active Player: A player who has money in the pot and has not folded his hand.

All In: Placing all of your remaining chips into the pot.

Back Door Flush or Straight: A flush or straight made by catching the last two cards to make the hand.

Bet: To voluntarily put money into the pot.

Bad Beat: When you have a good hand that is a favorite to win beaten by another hand.

Blinds: The large and small blinds are forced bets made before the first cards are dealt.

Board: The community cards turned face up in the middle of the table.

Call: To place money in the pot equal to the previous bet.

Calling Station: A player who will not fold his hand and will call all the pots to the river. This is a weak-passive player who rarely raises the pot. You will make your most money from this type of player.

Case Card: The fourth card of a certain rank. If you held two Kings and a third was showing on the board, the fourth King would be the case King.

Chop: When no players have called the blind bets and the two players in the blinds choose to take their bets back rather than to play out the hand.

Cold Call: To call a raise without having already called a bet.

Drawing Dead: Drawing to a hand that has no chance of winning.

Drowning on the River: Getting beat by a player who makes his hand with the river card.

Flop: The first three community cards turned over at the same time.

Fold: To cease play by throwing in your hand.

Hole Cards: Two cards dealt face down to be used as the players starting hand.

Muck: The pile of discarded and folded hands along with the burn cards. To muck your hand means to fold.

Nuts: The nuts is the best hand that can be made from the cards on the board and the cards in a player's hand. If you had an Ace high flush, you would have the nut flush.

Overcard: One or both of your pocket cards that are higher than any of the cards on the board.

Overpair: A pocket pair that is higher than any of the cards on the board.

Paint Card: Kings, Queens, and Jacks, also called face cards. You can easily spot a face card by the amount of colors and distinguish it from the other cards.

Pocket Cards: Your two cards that are dealt to you face down. Also known as hole cards.

Pot Odds: The relationship between the money in the pot versus the amount of money it will cost you to continue in the hand.

Rainbow: A flop that contains three cards of different suits.

Raise: To make a bet that is double the size of the bet made by the previous bettor.

River: The fifth and last community card turned over on the board.

Runner: When the turn and river card make a winning hand for a player that would have been a loser otherwise. See Back Door.

Set: Three of a kind when you have a pair in the pocket.

Showdown: At the end of the final round when all players remaining in the hand turn over their cards to determine the winner.

Side Pot: A pot that is formed after a player goes all in. This pot cannot be won by the all-in player.

Slowplay: To weakly play a strong hand by calling or checking instead of raising. This is done to conceal the strength of your hand.

Smooth Call: To call a bet rather than raise the pot.

Suited: Two cards in a starting hand that are the same suit. A flop consisting of three cards of the same suit would be a suited flop.

Trips: Three of a kind where a pair is on the board and the third card is one of your pocket cards.

Turn: The fourth community card turned over on the board.

Undercard: A card in your hand smaller than the highest card on the board.

Underpair: A pocket pair smaller than the lowest card on the board.

Winner: The type of player you aspire to be.

Index

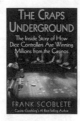

 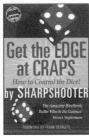